Mrs. Manders' Cook Book

Mrs. Manders' Cook Book

by Olga Sarah Manders

Edited by Rumer Godden

NEW YORK / THE VIKING PRESS

Published in 1968 by The Viking Press, Inc.
625 Madison Avenue, New York, N.Y. 10022

Library of Congress catalog card number: 68–22867

Printed in U.S.A.
Illustrations by David Knight

CONTENTS

v

Preface:

OLGA SARAH MANDERS

by Rumer Godden

She was in the village all the time.

It was a quiet East Sussex village and when we
came there from London we had found women who would
come in daily to help in the house, as we had found a dear,
elderly, methodical, never-to-be-hurried gardener. These we
had hoped for, expected, but we certainly had not expected a
Mrs. Manders, not only a cook but a chef, trained under
famous chefs, yet one who managed to combine her skills
with friendliness, a refreshing earthiness, good humour, and
love: love of people and animals, flowers, and all the gifts
of good food. "*Look* at this beautiful cabbage," she says,
as she might say, "Look at this beautiful painting." "Look
at the firmness and the colour. It's a little beauty and it still

has the dew on it, it's so fresh." The cabbage is probably
from her garden, grown by her husband, and part of her
praise of it comes from her loyalty and pride in him; for me
the important thing is that it will be just as beautiful when
it is cooked—and how few people can cook cabbage—crisp,
buttered, and invitingly green.

Mrs. Manders walked into our lives on one cold, dark
February evening; walked in through the back entrance, un-
announced, and knocked at my study door.

We were in a difficult patch, one of those known to all
professional women who work on exacting projects and yet
have families and homes. That November our Austrian
cook-housekeeper, on whom we relied, had been suddenly
called back to Austria to nurse her mother, who was mor-
tally ill. Why, oh why, we asked then, had we left London,
where a cook was not difficult to find, and come to live in
an isolated house in the country, where no one would con-
sent to come and work? All winter the tug of war between
writing and domesticity had gone on, tearing my work and
time—and me—into rags. That evening, putting the finishing touches to a chapter between dashes to the kitchen,
I was near despair. Then came that knock. "Who *is* it?"
I called impatiently.

In came a short, plump person wearing boots, mitts, and
such a large anorak with a fur-trimmed hood that she looked
like an Eskimo—but an Eskimo with fair hair and blue eyes
who beamed confidence and, better still, capability. She had
heard, she said, we were needing . . . We were indeed.

Mrs. Manders at that time was cook at the White Hart,
a well-known small inn on the marshes; but things were
quiet there in winter and they often "laid her off," so that
she thought she could squeeze us in.

"But can you come in the evening?" I asked doubtfully.

"Why not? I always did."

She had been cook for a while to Sheila Kaye-Smith and
her husband, Sir Penrose Fry, from whom we had bought
the house after Sheila Kaye-Smith died. Sheila Kaye-Smith's
best-known novel was the Sussex *Joanna Godden*; Godden

is a common Sussex and Kentish name but it was still strange that I, Rumer Godden, who had never known Sheila, should come to live in what had been her house. Mrs. Manders had loved her. "She was a gourmet," said Mrs. Manders in recommendation. "I enjoyed coming here."

I thought of our two miles' distance from the village— "There's a bus," said Mrs. Manders—the quarter-mile of dark and lonely drive. "I know this place like the back of my hand," said Mrs. Manders.

"But waiting in the lane, in the dark and cold, for the bus to take you home?" I said doubtfully.

Our bus service is erratic, depending on how many stops the driver makes, how many parcels he delivers personally, how long he stops to talk, but, "I have my torch," and, "I'll be in tomorrow," said Mrs. Manders. They seemed the most comforting words I had ever heard—and they were true. She was in the next day and the day and the week after that.

I understood, of course, that she would have to go back to the White Hart; cooking in a hotel was surely more rewarding than cooking for us. "Well, I don't know," said Mrs. Manders after a week or so more. "It's monotonous. Nowadays, it's mostly traffic people." The way she said "traffic" was withering. "They don't want my lovely dishes, just something out of the deep freeze: a grill, Dover sole, steak, duckling. They'll hardly wait till you chip the ice off it. That's not cooking"—and not eating, I could have said.

"But doesn't the inn want to work up a reputation?"

"The other pays best," said Mrs. Manders without rancour. "Now I thought for tomorrow we might have a nice bit of halibut, fresh, in a sauce with almonds. . . ." And there were to be tomorrows and tomorrows.

In England, before the Reformation, there was a belief that, even if the food was simple, the home poor, every time the table was laid for a meal it was a humble reflection of the Last Supper; food was holy, not in a ritualistic sense, but as a blessing from God. The churches too use homely ordinary things for the sacraments: water, salt, oil, and what the Church of England beautifully calls "creatures of bread and wine." These reverences seem lost in our lives today, yet still a belief persists—and I have heard doctors endorse it—that if food is cooked with care and love, and, however plain it is, served without haste and invitingly, there will be no indigestion or bad tempers in the family. This is true of Mrs. Manders' cooking; there is always a feeling of well-being and ease after her food, and she takes as much trouble cooking for us when we are alone as she does for a dinner party; her eyes light up, though, when a party is mooted, and she has often said wistfully, looking at a crab salad, a dish of beef olives, or her Chicken Louisette, "Isn't there *someone* you could ask? There ought to be more of you to enjoy it."

"But surely her cooking is very extravagant?" people say. Good food, of course, costs money, and Mrs. Manders cooks with the best ingredients she can find, but she is not extravagant; on the contrary she is far more frugal than most cooks are: every bit, snippet, and bone is kept: vegetable water goes into soups and sauces, as do cream gone sour and bacon rinds; the "ends" of red and white wine are hoarded in special bottles; leftover bread, potato peelings, outer cabbage and lettuce leaves are kept for the chickens. Nothing is wasted, and this is part of the reverence with which she treats things; it is this sense of values, of true appreciation, that marks her out.

It is not only appreciation of food and wine. In all the time she has been with us, Mrs. Manders has broken only one wineglass—and that was wrapped in a cloth so that she could not see it: her distress was immense. Nothing else has been as much as chipped—a chip, to me, is worse than a break; fine china, glass, and silver are safe in her hands; nothing under her care is lost or misused; it is a joy to see how, for instance, she looks after her knives; they are sharpened by herself, kept in a special drawer, and each tip is protected by a cork. She loves and can look after linen and embroidery, upholstery, clothes, polished furniture—but then a true artist has an instinctive understanding of other arts. Wasn't it Sir Osbert Sitwell's cook who used to advise him on modern painting? I am not surprised, because Mrs. Manders understands writing in a way many of my friends and relations do not. "You go on," she says to me when I am busy. "Leave everything to me." She knows, too, how drained and tired-out writing can make one. "I expect you feel like last week's groceries," she says in sympathy and, rare generosity in a good cook, she is not put out if I keep dinner waiting.

All this sounds as if she were a paragon, which is wrong because Mrs. Manders is far too human, too much of a person to be that, and, like the rest of us, she has human traits. "I'm a snob," she says and believes in being a snob with a tremendous veneration for birth and breeding—she can tell you as much about the royal family as anyone in England—but then, choosing beer for herself rather than sherry, she will say, "Proper common I am." She has human foibles too—she never misses her bus. The bus always "goes without her." Her "matelot" humour, as she calls it, can be broad, and she loves a gossip—though only with her peers —and she can get in a fuss, a really temperamental tizzy, if her cooking is impeded; but when she comes in every afternoon, goodness comes with her. Some of it is tangible: she always brings a basket, a cornucopia of a basket weighed down and overflowing, and what comes out of it! Or what doesn't come out of it! Newly picked peas—"They're so *young!*" Mrs. Manders will say in ecstasy—eggs from her own hens, a small haunch of lamb she has found in the market: "Look at it! Perfect! Far cheaper than at the butcher's!"

I remember once she had had the day off and gone into Hastings to shop and go to the hairdresser. She sailed in on her way back—"Just to bring you one or two things." Her hair had been set so that it was in small curls; she was wearing black trousers and a black sweater, a necklace of big pearls, pearl earrings, and gold shoes, and she still had the basket and was panting with its weight. "Look, a little guinea fowl. Sweet bacon . . . they had *such* lovely cheese . . . and these huge peaches."

Her husband, Mr. Manders, is often pressed into service and comes in with a live lobster he has bought off the fishing boats, or he brings his home-grown tomatoes. In sweet-pea time there are bunches of sweet peas, and in spring, lilies-of-the-valley. The big young fair-haired sailor son comes too, when his ship is home and he has leave; sometimes he comes to lend a hand, especially at Christmas —he is a naval chef—sometimes just to visit.

When our house was burned down, leaving us homeless and possessionless, so that for months, more than a year, we had to camp in furnished houses, Mrs. Manders still came, though the kitchens were awkward, the cookers sometimes dirty, the china poor with queer oddments of plate. I remember a trolley that had crooked casters so that it would not run—we called it "Mrs. Manders' cross"—but she made do without a grumble and the food was as good as ever, with a welcome for anybody who came: an American publisher or a French film director; the Indian tailor who, on a work permit, stayed with us to make new curtains and covers—for him Mrs. Manders cooked a vegetable curry every night. There are welcomes and heaps of food for our young and impecunious actor friends, for any and every friend, and always for daughters, grandchildren—and dogs.

One glad day Mrs. Manders and I went up to London to equip a new kitchen—a day divided between Harrods and Soho—though, as she said mournfully, "New saucepans and whisks and knives, however good, can never be the same as the old, trusty tools." We made a new kitchen in this centuries-old house in Rye, and now she and I, most evenings, are alone; the daily help and my secretary have gone home, my husband is at his club, if friends are coming to dinner they have not arrived; it is a peaceful time, fruitful for work, hers and mine. My study is on the floor above the kitchen, but I can hear Mrs. Manders. I like to hear her moving about, talking to the dogs, answering the telephone —she knows how to protect me, though when she talks on the telephone you can hear her from Rye to Hastings. "Can you really?" asks Mrs. Manders in dismay. "Well, you and the telephone have never been good friends," I console her. Often a wonderful smell will steal up the stairs, and sometimes, using the excuse that I am "stuck," I go down for a taste or a tidbit—though there is often a plate I am not allowed to touch, a plate of special little sausage rolls with a label on them saying, "For Mr. Haynes-Dixon." Now and again I stop to try and learn how to beat a soufflé properly or shape butter or make a sauce, but I am a complete duffer at these and usually end by listening to her stories. One evening I said, "Mrs. Manders, you know, you ought to write a book."

"A book!"

She turned in astonishment from the stove, a saucepan in one hand, a wooden spoon in the other. "A book! Good Lord!" she said—but did not, as I noticed, stop her stirring for a moment. "Me write a book!"

"Why not?" And, spurred by the thought, I said, "I'll buy you a fountain pen and you can start straight away."

Perhaps it was the pen, perhaps it was just Mrs. Manders, but bit by bit a book emerged. I have helped a little to shape her ideas into a plan and, here and there, to clarify her exposition, but the style and prose are her own, a mixture of simplicity and sound tradition, as unmistakably Mrs. Manders as her cooking.

"But what sort of a book *is* it?" she asked when it was done.

I said, "A cook book, of course," and this is it.

Part One

A widow has cold pie—nurse gives you cake,
From gen'rous merchants ham or sturgeon take;
The farmer has brown bread as fresh as day,
And butter fragrant as the dew of May,
Cornwall squab pie, and Devon white pot brings,
And Lei'ster beans and bacon, food for kings.

—"The Art of Cooking"

WHY I AM I

There is one question everybody asks me: "Mrs.
Manders, how did you learn to cook like this?" The answer
is: "Not in five minutes—and not only by cooking." Char-
acter, heredity, and training have a great deal to do with it.
I come from a long line of naval ancestors and can trace
their association with the sea back to the days of Nelson—
and what does the sea give you? Health and a wide vision
as well as thoroughness, neatness, and cleanliness. There
is a legend that good cooks cook in a wonderful muddle;
all I can say is, if they do, they were not brought up in the
Navy.

My father, who served with the Royal Navy for twenty-
four years, was a disciplinarian; everything in our household

had to be done in a shipshape fashion; that is my fashion still, and I will not tolerate mess in the kitchen. My mother was also strict, and she ordained, when I left school, that there was to be no nonsense such as to whether I wanted to "take up" this or that. I was to go, as she put it, into "good service."

My grandmother and aunts were horrified, especially Grandmother. I remember her as a very gentle soul; she had had a refined upbringing and was quite a lady, nothing like my boisterous grandfather, who always acted as if he were an officer on the quarterdeck; but Grandmother spoke her mind now: "Send Olga away to service! Turning your only daughter into a hewer of wood and a drawer of water!"

Grandmother had quite a turn of phrase, but in spite of all objections I was sent away, into a large household in Kensington Square in London, three hundred and sixty miles from home—my father, by then retired from the Navy, was a coast guard in Pembrokeshire in Wales. You can imagine how homesick I was! I could have cried my eyes out every night, except that I knew my father would have been ashamed of me.

I was green and callow and so had to start as fourth housemaid and went through a gruelling time under the dragon of a head housemaid, Amy. Dragon or not, I must thank Amy because she trained me thoroughly. Above stairs she was called by her surname, but to myself I called her "the Lincoln Imp." In Lincoln Cathedral there is a famous sculpture of the imp, an ugly, spiteful small devil. Amy came from Lincoln, and she was ugly and spiteful. I was not allowed to use my own name, Olga; "Mary" was considered more suitable, and Amy stressed that I was never to be seen by my employers. Woe betide me if I went through the green baize door that separated our quarters from theirs.

Amy kept me at her heels from the time I got up, 6 a.m., till I was sent to bed, punctually at 9 p.m. I had only one half-day off a week.

The task I hated most was the cleaning of the housemaids' pantry sink; it was made of shining copper, and every afternoon when the maids had finished, I had to restore that sink to brightness with salt, sand, and vinegar and leave it completely dry; if it was the slightest bit damp, Amy would fetch me to do it again.

Then I had to rush up to my room to wash and change into afternoon uniform and rush down again to the servants' hall to lay the servants' afternoon tea; I used to feel sorry for the kitchen and scullery maids because they did not change out of their print dresses—and I looked down a little on them too. I did not guess that I should soon be following in their steps.

In my estimation Bates, the butler, was a very grand person, tall, dignified, and fatherly-looking. All of us were in awe of him except—I remarked—Cook, who treated him as an equal; they used to eat together in her sanctum. Every other Sunday I would have to wait on him as he took in or removed the courses at dinner in the dining room, and he would give me little tidbits, Scotch salmon or pheasant. I remember when two or three brace of pheasant arrived from the family's country estate, Amy's calling out, "Bates! Bates! The cocks and hens have arrived."

She could be jovial, too jovial. When I was new, I was too innocent to realize that Amy was "on the bottle." The family used to go away, leaving us on board wages; then Amy would have long drinking sessions with Bates in his pantry, where he would sit most of the day reading the racing news. When she was drunk, Amy would get into terrible tempers which scared me to death; sometimes she was violent.

Looking back, I think somehow I got under Amy's skin, perhaps because my parents used to send me money to augment my wages of one pound, eight shillings and fourpence a month. She did not like my having the extra money, nor did she like my manners, which, as I had been carefully brought up, were good, and she was jealous of Bates's kindness to me. When he gave me tidbits he always said, "Don't let Amy know."

She often drove me to tears and a young girl's despair, but it was eighteen months before my mother thought I had learned enough to come home. On the long train journey I felt as if I had been released from a cage, but oddly enough, no sooner was I settled at home again than I was restless, and this time I was the one who decided what I should do and where I should go. I remember I thought a great deal about the cook at Kensington Square; after Bates, she had been the most important person on the domestic side of the family, queen in her own territory, with no need to kowtow * to anyone, and I soon decided that I, Olga Sarah, would be a cook—I did not know then what the word "chef" meant—but not only would I cook for gentlemen like our master in the Square, I would cook for a prince or an earl and I would travel to America.

I was in a rosy dream, but a cook, as I said, isn't made in five minutes—or a day, or a year. Once more I travelled to London and started the hard way, as scullery maid in a West End mansion.

When I arrived, the kitchenmaid, Emily, immediately took me under her wing and made me feel at home, a good thing because when she brought me to the chef, André, a tall fierce-looking man, he snapped question after question at me, first impressing on me that I was to ask *him* no questions! Emily, he said, would tell me all I wanted to know. Now I met my old enemy sand, salt, and vinegar again because under Emily's supervision I had to clean and scour all the cooking utensils, which meant day after day of dirty, greasy pans and pudding bowls, basins and fry pans, spoons, wooden boards, mortars and pestles. Sometimes I felt I had grease up to my elbows; my hands got chapped and stained and my nails stubbed, while my back ached from standing at the sink—I believe I used to have night-

* Mrs. Manders often interlards her conversation with words borrowed from her sailor father, husband, and son; by contrast she has a "refined" sort of English, taught her by that ladylike grandmother and the butlers, ladies' maids, and chefs she used to work with; then suddenly she breaks into some expressive earthy phrase: "I've got the screws," "I'm dying upwards," and, describing a very talkative woman, "Mrs. Jaw-me-dead."—R.G.

mares about saucepans—but I learned, thoroughly and carefully from the very bottom of the ladder, how to respect and care for the least of cooking things.

I also had to clean and blacklead the huge coal range in the kitchen, polishing its steel corners and hasps with wire wool, and, worst of all, keep it stoked; morning, noon, and evening found me shovelling coal, and I used to think it had the largest and hungriest mouth on earth. In hot weather the heat from the monster was terrific, especially when I had to draw boiling water from the brilliantly polished tap on the side. I had to endure these huge coal ranges all the years of my apprenticeship, and I remember what a revelation it was when, years later, I met my first Aga; it was heaven to be able to cook in comfort and exactness, refueling only twice a day! Since then I have had gas and electric cookers, once even an oil stove, but an Aga is far the best.

Under Emily's supervision I was shown how to clean and prepare vegetables properly, to wash them carefully, removing every speck of dirt, and dry them. André, whom I called "sir," said I was making slow but good progress, and presently I not only washed vegetables but helped Emily to cook them. It gave me great pleasure when André allowed me to wait on him, though he used to tease me by speaking to me in French, shaking his head, saying, "She will never make a cook, that one!" All the same, as I gained confidence he let me make a few simple things for the staff, who were kind and said I was doing fine.

When the family went away to their country estate, about six of us staff, including the cook and butler, were left in the London house on board wages, which meant our monthly wages were paid as usual and we were given in cash fifteen shillings a week to enable us to buy our own food; André used to superintend the cooking of this. Being so young, I was not a very efficient manager and on several occasions found myself stony broke without a Sunday dinner, but the other members of the staff usually came to my rescue.

Once I bought a large rasher of gammon for my own

dinner, and André asked me how I was going to cook it. "Just grill it," I said, but André laughed at me and said, "My little cabbage, I'll teach you how to make your adorable gammon rasher into a perfect meal," and he did.

ANDRÉ'S SPECIAL GAMMON RASHER

1 slice ham, ½ inch thick, about 1 lb.
2 tablespoons sugar
2 tablespoons butter
2 tablespoons flour
2 tablespoons wine vinegar
1 tablespoon chopped chives
1 teaspoon tomato purée
salt to taste
1¼ cups stock (preferably chicken)

METHOD: Broil the ham and keep it hot. Brown the sugar in a saucepan over medium heat; do not let it burn. Add the butter, then the flour, mix together, and slowly add the other ingredients. Cook all together slowly for 20 minutes, stirring all the time. Pour over the ham. Serves 2.

Of course André was waited on hand and foot by both Emily and me, and I used to think, One day I'll be like that.

After two years Emily left, and I was promoted to kitchenmaid. "Kitchenmaid" does not sound like much, but it can open vistas to an intelligent girl, and I believe I was such. André saw how proud I was and used to call me "Madame."

My first sweet, which he had trained me in making, was sent to the dining room on his day out. It was a hot ice cream which we called Flaming Surprise.

FLAMING SURPRISE

6 macaroons
12 ladyfingers
a little brandy or Grand Marnier to soak the
    biscuits
6 egg whites

> 2½ tablespoons sugar
> 1 pint coffee ice cream, very hard
> sugar for sprinkling
> 2½ tablespoons brandy or Grand Marnier

METHOD: Soak macaroons and ladyfingers in brandy or Grand Marnier until they are quite soft, about 20 minutes. Line a heatproof dish, either metal or glass, with these; the dish should be larger than the shape of the ice cream and have straight or sloping sides 2 to 3 inches deep. Beat egg whites until very stiff; fold in 2 tablespoons sugar.

Preheat oven to 450°. Five minutes before the dessert is to be eaten, put on top of the soaked ladyfingers and macaroons the coffee ice cream, which must be rock-hard. Cover quickly and completely with the beaten egg whites and sprinkle with sugar.

Put the whole dish *at once* into the very hot oven, just long enough, 2 to 3 minutes, to brown white of egg before the ice cream melts. Meanwhile heat the brandy or Grand Marnier.

Hurry dish to table, pour the warmed brandy or Grand Marnier over it, and set alight. Serves 8 to 10.

Was my face flaming when it went in! But I had compliments from upstairs.

André also excelled in sauce-making—the most difficult of all being Hollandaise Sauce.

HOLLANDAISE SAUCE

> 2 egg yolks
> 2½ tablespoons heavy cream
> ½ teaspoon tarragon vinegar
> pinch of salt
> 4 tablespoons softened butter
> 1 tablespoon lemon juice
> additional salt and pepper to taste

METHOD: Put the egg yolks, cream, and vinegar, with a pinch of salt, into the top of a double boiler. Stir this continuously over simmering water, using a wooden spoon, until mixture thickens. Do not let it boil, as boiling will cause it to curdle. Remove from heat; cut the butter into small pieces, and add them, one at a time, waiting until each piece has melted. Stir constantly. Add the lemon juice and season to taste.

If this mixture is too thick or if it curdles, a few drops of water stirred in will usually remedy it. Makes about ⅔ cup.

But I eventually conquered this sauce too.

André showed me how to cut and prepare meat and how to care for knives; now I have my own knives and take them with me wherever I go.

On my birthday one year, with my employer's approval, André took me out to dinner, a special treat indeed! The daughter of the house had a dress made for me, a simple little dress of real shantung silk, natural-coloured, with a sash of cornflower-blue velvet. We went in a taxi to the Savoy and, like the connoisseur he was, André explained all the dishes to me. It was the grandest occasion—and one of the happiest evenings—of my life.

After three years I felt I could really tackle a cook's post, but my parents saw further than I did; they had been pleased by my patience, steadiness, and determination, and now they offered to send me to Marshall's School of Cookery for nine months, where I learned more advanced cooking. From there I went to a domestic-science college. Then I went to the Dorchester and Park Lane Hotels to learn omelette- and soufflé-making under the chefs.

I vividly remember my first sight of the kitchen at the Dorchester; I was bewildered by its vastness and the number of figures in white caps. There was a bevy of different chefs, and round each was his smaller bevy of assistants. One chef was so tall that his cap reached the ceiling; he developed a permanent stoop. Sometimes a flame would shoot up so that I thought a pan was on fire; but worst of all was the noise, the hissing and bubbling and sizzling, the stockpot simmering away, the sound of the chefs' boots on the tiled floor, and the way some of the chefs swore and shouted at their assistants. *"Imbécile! Imbécile!"* seemed the most common word. I was used to quiet and consideration, and the noise, the impatience, the brilliant light and heat helped to frighten me almost into a useless puppet. Every night when I left, I felt I could not face the bedlam again—and every morning I went back.

Of course the heat was terribly trying for the chefs, especially when there was pressure from a rush of orders. Each man seemed continually to be wiping his face with his kerchief and often his white coat and blue checked trousers were damp with sweat. The black stoves, numbers of them, were in the middle of the room, which I thought odd until I saw how conveniently one could work on all sides of them. Everyone spoke French, and even when I was under his tuition my particular chef, Monsieur Paul, would speak only French to me; he seemed to believe he could make me understand by signs and nods. Miraculously, he did, but for a long time I felt an interloper and an ignoramus.

The hours were long, from ten in the morning until two in the afternoon and starting again at five o'clock; we were supposed to finish at ten, but more often than not it was midnight. Paul, though, was a beautiful cook and one of his specialties was Omelette au Kümmel.

OMELETTE AU KÜMMEL

> 1 tablespoon tomato purée
> 2 teaspoons finely granulated sugar
> 4 eggs
> 1 tablespoon butter
> 1 tablespoon sugar
> ⅓ cup Kümmel, warmed

METHOD: Mix tomato purée with 2 teaspoons fine sugar and beat. Whisk up the eggs and 1 tablespoon water until fluffy. Melt the butter in the omelette pan; when it is really hot and sizzling, pour in gently the beaten eggs. As soon as the eggs set underneath, keep tilting the pan and lifting the omelette around the edges with a spatula, so as to allow the liquid on top to run underneath and cook. When eggs are almost set, put the hot tomato jam into the centre. Fold over.

Place the omelette in a hot serving dish, sprinkle 1 tablespoon sugar over it, and put it under a hot broiler for 3 minutes.

Remove, and pour the previously warmed Kümmel over the omelette. Now set it alight. Be careful to keep the flame alive by stirring it with a spoon, otherwise the flavour of Kümmel will be overpowering. Prick the omelette now and again with a fork. The flame must die out naturally in spite of the constant stirring. Serve at once. Serves 3 to 4.

At the Park Lane I was senior to some apprentices, being by now quite experienced and, of course, older, so that more was entrusted to me. I had, too, got used to working in noise and was beginning to understand the routine. There was more camaraderie here, and the chefs seemed a little less pressed, though there was still the incessant hurry, waiters and commies, the young "learning" waiters, rushing in and out, so that at times it seemed as if hell was let loose. I was there to learn the art of soufflé-making and had to start with the fundamentals. The chef gave me a heavy wire beater to beat up the eggs by hand; at first I was so slow and awkward with it that I nearly gave up, but after days of my struggling with the mass of yellow yolks and with the whites, the chef succeeded in teaching me how to hold that gigantic brute beater—it was just a matter of using the wrist with the right rhythm—and I learned a light rhythmical beat that has stood me in good stead ever since; no electrical beater can equal it.

At the Park Lane, in those days, the head chef's specialty was Turbot Soufflé.

TURBOT SOUFFLÉ

1 ½-lb. slice turbot, or halibut
2 tablespoons butter
2 tablespoons flour
⅔ cup fish stock
¼ cup heavy cream
3 eggs, separated
1 tablespoon white wine
salt and pepper to taste

METHOD: Preheat oven to 375°. Put turbot or halibut in a heavy pan with water to cover, bring to a simmer, and poach over low heat for about 15 minutes. Drain fish while warm, reserving the stock, and remove bones and skin; flake into nice pieces and keep until required. Butter a 1-quart soufflé dish. Melt butter in pan and add flour; mix well, but do not let get brown. Now add to this fish stock and cream. Cook over low heat for 10 minutes, stirring all the time. Remove pan from heat and beat in egg yolks, which should be at room temperature, one by one. Stir in the wine and add the flaked fish. Mix gently and season to taste. Lastly beat the egg whites until stiff and fold them in. Pour into the buttered soufflé dish and bake for 45 minutes or until the soufflé has risen. Serve at once. Serves 4.

This is a very delicately flavoured dish which gives satisfaction to all. I am always complimented on it.

Sometimes late at night in the Park Lane, when things began to quieten and there were pauses in which we could talk, the boys used to try and scare me by telling me that when the place was empty rats would come and take away the eggs; one rat, they said, would lie on its back holding the egg, and the others would pull him along by his tail. I never saw this feat.

This was my training, from first to last almost six years, years full of hard work and hard lessons; hardest to learn was patience: patience to beat a cake properly, to allow the three days needed to make a good oxtail stew, to prepare crêpes suzette, to peel a pound of grapes one by one, to hull broad beans from their outer skin—in fact, to be thorough. At the end I had the feeling I was properly, thoroughly qualified, more than ready to take my first post.

PEOPLE—AND PLACES
WHERE I HAVE COOKED

It is not given to many people to realize one of their two fondest dreams—I still have the other, which is to go to America—but then perhaps most people's dreams are not within their capabilities. Luckily mine, to be a first-class cook, was within my power, and I certainly worked hard for it, but it did not come true all at once; there were disappointments first.

The day came when I knew without a doubt that I was ready to take my first post, no matter how exacting it might be. I looked forward to being on my own, with full responsibility, and I got a place in London through the old Regina Bureau in Grosvenor Street.

In later times I was to become a steady client of the

Regina; I grew to know it as it knew me, and when in after years I pushed open the glass door and saw the long counter and the grey-haired clerks working at it with letters and telephones, it felt quite homelike, but that first time I was very nervous when I took my place among the line of domestics waiting. I had to go up to the counter, say what sort of post I wanted, and produce my references. "None as head cook?" asked the woman.

"I haven't started yet," I wanted to say, but thought it better to point out there were plenty as cook-assistant, from Monsieur André, the Dorchester, the Park Lane, and so on, and that I was fully qualified. The clerk was severe, and quite rightly; a domestic agency builds up a reputation, and the Regina would not take just anyone on its lists.

The agency vetted the domestics thoroughly; it was not so easy to vet the employers, though when servants were continually leaving a place, the agency soon got to know why and that employer was put on its blacklist.

In later days, when a clerk showed me her list of available posts, if something appealed to me I would pick it out and she would telephone for an appointment. I would then go off by taxi if the post was in London, or by train to the country, to be interviewed. I wonder if the employer knew how minutely she was being interviewed too. Though I hope I looked as if I were keeping my eyes to myself, they would be taking in everything; the sound, too, of her voice and the way she laughed—or did not laugh—told volumes. [I wonder what Mrs. Manders made of me. Presumably I passed.—R.G.]

After the interview I would be given my expenses and would go home to await a letter. If we were both "suited," the agency would take a fee, twelve shillings and sixpence to fifteen shillings, from me, and from my employer a percentage based on my first month's wages.

On two occasions I was sent to places where I immediately sensed that things were not as they should be. How I knew this is difficult to explain, but I immediately took a quick and, I hope, dignified departure. This first time, though, the house to which I was sent seemed thoroughly respectable, as indeed it was—almost too much so.

It was a small household, husband, wife, and one daughter, all strangely old-fashioned and quiet, who lived very plainly and never entertained. There I was, all agog, wanting to do my utmost with my carefully acquired skills, and what was asked of me? Almost nothing. Not one of my lovely dishes was allowed; there was the plainest and dullest of food, except on Sunday, and that was worst of all because every Sunday the same thing was ordered, jugged hare, a dish I thoroughly dislike. Experienced cook though I am, I still shrink from drawing and preparing game and, of all game, especially hare; I gave the gardener's boy packet after packet of cigarettes to cut up these horrors for me. The whole house was run in a gloomy, parsimonious way; my dream of kitchen and scullery maids to help me came down to a daily woman who had an impediment in her speech and whose wages were small because she was dim-witted; the poor creature had such a squint that I could never tell if she was looking at me or not.

Everything I used had to be weighed and accounted for; butter was rationed, cream or wine for cooking was unheard of, as were herbs or spices. Every day brought the same dull routine; every night everyone went to bed early, the master having locked all the doors and windows and collected the silver in a basket to take up with him. There was neither laughter nor cheerful talking in that house, and I, a young woman, felt as if the depression and disappointment were covering me like mould, but I didn't want to leave too soon; it was my first post, and a good reference is important to a young cook. To this day I cannot look at jugged hare without a shudder, but here is my recipe (of course I use wine!).

JUGGED HARE

1 hare, 3-4 lbs., cleaned
flour for dredging hare
4 tablespoons butter
6 slices bacon

salt and cayenne pepper
bouquet garni (see index)
1 onion, peeled
3 cloves
2 teaspoons grated lemon peel
6 peppercorns
1¼ cups claret
1¼ cups meat stock or gravy
2 teaspoons flour
a few more drops of claret
1¼ tablespoons red-currant jelly
⅓ cup port wine

METHOD: Cut cleaned hare into pieces, dredge them with flour. Melt butter in a large heavy-bottomed pan, put in pieces of hare, and sauté until nice and brown. Lay slices of bacon, to counteract the dryness of the hare, in bottom of a stewpan, then pack in the pieces of browned hare. Sprinkle with a seasoning of salt and a very little cayenne pepper. Now put in the bouquet garni, an onion stuck with the cloves, grated lemon peel, and six peppercorns. Moisten with the 1¼ cups of claret and the stock or gravy. Bring to a boil, then cover tightly and simmer on low heat until hare is tender, 1½ to 2 hours. Remove hare and put in a bowl over a saucepan of boiling water to keep hot. Strain gravy. Mix 2 teaspoons flour smooth in a little claret, add red-currant jelly. Boil gravy, stir in flour mixture, add port. Put hare into gravy to heat thoroughly. Dish up; garnish with forcemeat balls and fried croûtons (see index). Serves 6.

FORCEMEAT BALLS

6 tablespoons white breadcrumbs
¼ teaspoon grated lemon peel
¼ teaspoon mixed herbs
1 tablespoon chopped parsley
4 tablespoons finely chopped suet
2 tablespoons finely chopped lean bacon
salt and pepper to taste
1 egg
melted butter

METHOD: Mix breadcrumbs with lemon peel, herbs, suet, bacon, and seasoning. Bind all this with one raw egg and roll into balls the size of marbles. Sauté in melted butter.

Perhaps this experience gave me a fright, because for a while I took only temporary posts, travelling up and down the length and breadth of the country and meeting all sorts of interesting people. There was a break in my career when I married a Jewish boy, a nephew of Ada Reeve, who in her young days was one of the Gaiety girls. The family was kindly disposed towards me, though I was a goy, and they gave me an insight into Jewish ways and cooking. However, the marriage was not happy, in fact it broke up after six years, and for me it was back to the Regina and work.

After a time I gained my Cordon Bleu and built up a repertoire of menus and dishes to which, as with all real cooks, I believed I could give a touch of my own. [You can indeed.—R.G.] All the while, too, I was getting to know some of the master chefs who became my friends and were very kind to me.

Raymond, chef on the *Train Bleu* for quite a while, kept me entertained with stories of some of the travellers. One of his specialties was Faisan à la Romanoff.

FAISAN À LA ROMANOFF

1 pheasant, 3½-4 lbs.
paprika, salt, pepper
3 oz. cream cheese
4 tablespoons butter
1 tablespoon cooking oil
⅓ cup vodka
2 to 3 teaspoons paprika
½ bay leaf
1 shallot, cut in half
⅓ cup Malaga or sherry
¾ lb. mushrooms, sliced
2 slices white bread
butter for sautéing bread
⅔ cup cream

METHOD: Dust inside of pheasant with salt, pepper, and a little paprika, then put in the cheese. Put 4 tablespoons butter and 1 tablespoon oil into a heavy pan and brown pheasant all over slowly; it must be well browned, but do not let the butter get black. Add salt and pepper and put in the vodka, light it, and when the flame has gone out add 2 to 3 teaspoonfuls paprika, according to your taste, the bay leaf, and shallot.

Cover pan and simmer for ½ hour, adding the wine at intervals, little by little. Put the mushrooms in the pan, cover, and simmer on until the pheasant is done, ½ to ¾ hour, according to age and weight. Test with fork to tell doneness.

Meanwhile cut the bread into rounds and sauté in butter until golden-brown. Remove bird from pan, place it on the bread on a serving dish, and keep hot. Put contents of the pan through a sieve, taste and readjust the seasoning, put pan back on heat, and stir in cream. Bring to the boil while whisking all the time. If sauce is too thick, add a little more Malaga or sherry. Pour a little sauce over the pheasant and serve the rest in a sauceboat. Serves 4.

This he had served at times to various royal travellers. He was left-handed (as I am) and told me that left-handed people (or cooks) made the best carvers.

Another friend, Signor Pogliocci, had a small, scrupulously clean Italian restaurant in Charlotte Street; the restaurant was always packed, as the food was exceptionally good. The kitchen was upstairs and, like the rest, was clean, small, and compact. It amazed me to see how easily the orders were dealt with; nothing was ever warmed up, each order being made with fresh items. The staff even made the bread, which, served fresh in baskets, was out of this world.

Signor Pogliocci taught me his version of the famous soup Minestrone.

MINESTRONE

½ lb. salt pork cut in small pieces
1 tablespoon cooking oil
1 large onion, chopped
1½ to 2 cups finely shredded white or green
   cabbage
1 cup finely shredded lettuce
¾ cup chopped celery (1 large stalk)
⅓ cup chopped carrot (1 large carrot)
1 cup peeled and quartered tomatoes
1 cup shelled peas (or ½ package frozen peas)
½ cup chopped green beans
2 teaspoons salt
¼ teaspoon pepper
½ cup ditalini (or any small pasta)

METHOD: In a large kettle (at least 5-quart) that can be covered, sauté pork in the cooking oil until slightly browned. Add onion and sauté until golden. Add 10 cups cold water and bring to the boil. Then add cabbage, lettuce, celery, carrot, tomatoes, peas, beans, and salt and pepper. Cover and simmer for 1½ hours. At this point cooking may be stopped until 20 minutes before serving when you add the pasta and bring soup up to the simmer again. Serve very hot, with a dish of grated Parmesan cheese to be passed at the table. Serves 8 to 12.

Madame Bertorelli, of Charlotte Street too, was famous for her Zabaglione Romana.

ZABAGLIONE ROMANA

1 fresh egg per person
1 heaping tablespoon sifted confectioner's
   sugar per person
about 2 tablespoons Marsala per person

METHOD: Break the eggs into the top of a double boiler; add the sugar. Put china cups (one per person) to warm.

Measure out the Marsala by using an eggshell, so that there is, more or less, the same amount of wine as egg.* Put the Marsala into the pan with the eggs and sugar. With a light wire whisk, whisk all together while the pan is on very low heat. Be sure it does not get too hot, or the mixture will curdle. As soon as the mixture thickens, in about 10 minutes, it is ready. Put quickly into warm cups and serve immediately.

Important: This must be served as soon as it is ready, or it will collapse. It cannot be kept waiting, so do not start to cook until within 10 minutes of its being wanted.

I had met the chef Marcel when I was at the Park Lane. Marcel was a perfectionist in all ways. One thing he insisted on, absolute quiet while he was "brooding," as he put it; no one must speak to him until he looked up and gave a half-bow. One of his best dishes was Les Oiseaux de Veau.

LES OISEAUX DE VEAU

4 escalopes of veal
pinch of basil
6 black peppercorns, crushed
4 anchovy fillets
3 shallots
5 tomatoes
6 large mushrooms
⅓ cup dry white wine
1 bay leaf
salt
1 teaspoon arrowroot

METHOD: Trim escalopes and flatten; sprinkle over each a little basil and crushed peppercorns. Put an anchovy fillet on each escalope, roll it up tightly like a sausage, and tie with thread.

Slice shallots, skin and slice tomatoes, slice the mushrooms. Melt the butter in a broad pan or flameproof casserole that can be covered, and gently sauté shallots; add the mushrooms and continue to sauté for 3 or 4 minutes. Add the tomatoes and lay

---

* If you find this difficult, break the eggs into a measuring jug, and then measure out an equal quantity of Marsala.

the escalopes on top. Pour in the wine, add bay leaf and rest of the peppercorns, season very lightly with salt. Cover, simmer for 20 minutes. Five minutes before serving, thicken the sauce lightly with arrowroot mixed in a little water. Serves 4.

Marcel had a charming wife, very good-looking, an Italian. I used sometimes to go to tea at their flat, and Maria would take me round Soho, to different shops where she was well known, and introduce me; in this way I got to know how to buy Italian commodities. My favourite shop was, and is, Parmigiani in Old Compton Street. I would feast my eyes on the different pastas, sausages, cheeses, every kind of dried beans; it was a fairyland to me, and Mrs. Parmigiani always found time to help me choose the best things. Some of these shopkeepers have died, some have retired or moved away, but they made Soho like a Mecca to me then and, with all its changes, I still love it.

Occasionally, on a Sunday, I would go with Marcel and Maria to the French church to Mass, a lovely experience which I enjoyed. Then some Sunday evenings they would take me to Saint Dominic's Priory, Hampstead, for Vespers; the singing was superb, and I would pray that I might succeed in my career—single-minded I was!—and these prayers were answered.

One afternoon the Regina Bureau telephoned to say that the Dowager Countess of Warwick needed a cook and this might be the place for me. I was interviewed in London and a few days later found myself, nervous but thrilled, travelling up to the Midlands. The grey-golden Warwick Castle was built at the top of a gentle hill and was entered by a drawbridge. Round it was what seemed a mile of parkland, beautifully kept; the back rooms looked down on the River Avon, where the swans glided on the gentle flow; it all seemed tranquil and beautiful.

Inside, the castle was vast; on certain days the state rooms were open to the public, but although I was impressed by the tapestries and armour I really had eyes only for my kitchen. Here was my kingdom—or queendom—at last!

The kitchen was spacious, light, and airy, the big table in the centre scrubbed to immaculate whiteness every morning by the little scullery maid, Violet—there was no formica in those days. She had to keep the monster black stove bright too, stoking it and carrying coal just as I had done. That stove was an excellent servant and cooked things beautifully. All round the walls were huge dressers, hung and set out with copper utensils; these, down to the smallest *dariole* mould, were embossed with the family crest. They were kept shining by the scullery maids and kitchenmaids with the same old vinegar, sand, and salt. On the window sill was a heavy iron box with a lid. This was the cake-box or glorified cake-tin; the cakes I made for the family often came out from the drawing-room with only one slice or two taken out of them, but they never went back. Fresh cakes were made, and the hardly touched ones went into the cake-box for the staff.

At half past seven each morning my kitchenmaid, Evelyn, would wake me with an early-morning tea-tray. I had my own bathroom and bed-sitting room, furnished very nicely. When I came down in my freshly laundered coat—a clean one every day—I would find Evelyn cooking the staff breakfast while Violet laid the table in the servants' hall. When I had had my breakfast, at the head of the table, I would come back to the kitchen to cook breakfast for the dining room. I gave the girls their orders for the day, then made up my dinner menu, which I had to submit to the Countess. She would often send for me to come to her boudoir, where we would talk the dishes over; she always asked me to sit down.

It was a busy life with all the planning and ordering as well as the cooking. I had to interview the head gardener and the dairyman—almost everything except meat and fish came from the Home Farm—but I had often to go into the town to choose and order personally, as I prefer to do. Besides the family and the large staff, there were many guests, at weekends especially, and in the summer there were big house parties, each gentleman or lady arriving with his own valet or maid, so that "above and below stairs" were hives of industry.

Sometimes the maids would let me peep at their ladies going down to dinner in their beautiful dresses, scented and groomed, jewels sparkling on their bare necks and arms.

I was proud of those dinners. When the family was alone, or there were only a few guests, they used the "small dining room" but this was still a wonderful room, oak-panelled, with superb carpets. Sometimes I was shown the table laid for a party, with the silver candelabra, the flowers—dark red roses or carnations and tuberoses grown in the castle greenhouses—the exquisite napery setting off the deep blue and gold of the porcelain. I would write the menus out in French on upright china blocks. [She has very clear writing. I envy her.—R.G.] The butler put them on the table. This is one of those menus:

MENU

Pomponettes de Foie Gras

Fresh Salmon Mousse

Green Salad

Roast Duckling with Cumberland Sauce

Fresh Garden Peas

Malakoff

Dessert

Coffee

POMPONETTES DE FOIE GRAS

½ lb. puff pastry (see index)
1 4-oz. tin or jar of pâté de foie gras
24 pistachio nuts, blanched, skinned, trimmed
fat for frying

METHOD: Roll pastry out thin and cut into 24 round pieces, 3 to 4 inches in diameter. Put 1 teaspoon foie gras in the centre of the pastry, and in the centre of this a pistachio nut. Fold pastry over and pinch together. Fry in deep fat (375°) for 3 to 4 minutes. Serve on a folded napkin and garnish with fried parsley. Yield: 24 appetizers.

SALMON MOUSSE

> 1 lb. salmon
> salt and pepper
> 1 tablespoon gelatine
> 5 tablespoons mayonnaise (see index)
> 2 rounded tablespoons finely chopped
>   cucumber
> ½ cucumber, sliced, for garnish
> a few cooked shelled prawns *
> squeeze of lemon juice
> lettuce leaves

METHOD: Cook salmon in barely simmering salted water just to cover, for 10 minutes, and leave in stock for a further 20 minutes. Make up aspic by dissolving gelatine over low heat in 2½ cups stock in which the salmon has been cooked. Leave to cool.

Remove spin and bones from salmon, then mix the salmon in a bowl with the mayonnaise and chopped cucumber. When aspic just begins to set, put a few slices of cucumber at the bottom of a fish-shaped dish or mould, arrange a few prawns round these, and cover thinly with some of the aspic. Put this in the freezing compartment of the refrigerator for a few minutes while stirring into the prepared salmon the remaining aspic, lemon juice, and seasoning. Remove mould from refrigerator and pour the mixture over the bottom layer. Chill thoroughly until set. Turn out onto a serving dish and surround with crisp lettuce leaves. Serves 4.

GREEN SALAD

> crisp lettuce leaves
> watercress sprigs
> 1 cucumber
> 1 clove garlic, crushed
> dressing (see index)

* Use large shrimp.

METHOD: Wash and thoroughly dry lettuce; trim watercress; peel cucumber and draw the tines of a fork down the sides, making grooves until cucumber is serrated; slice. Rub a wooden salad bowl with the clove of garlic. Put in the prepared salad. At the time of serving, sprinkle on the dressing and toss.

ROAST DUCKLING
WITH CUMBERLAND SAUCE

1 good duckling, 3 to 4 lbs.
salt and pepper
3 navel oranges
8 lumps of sugar
Cumberland sauce (see index)
watercress sprigs

METHOD: Preheat oven to 350°. Prepare duckling as follows: cut off the tips of wings and foot part of the legs; season inside with salt and pepper. Cut one orange in half and rub vigorously all over the bird, squeezing out as much juice over it as you can. Put these two halves of orange inside the duck. Tie string three times round duck; cut another orange into four slices and insert these under the string. Place bird on a rack in a roasting pan and roast for 1½ hours. Fifteen minutes before the bird is done, remove string and orange slices so that the breast browns evenly.

The third orange should be prepared while the duck is cooking; peel and remove all pith, cut into wafer-thin slices, remove seeds, and put slices into a sauce boat. Make a syrup with eight lumps of sugar boiled for 15 minutes in ½ cup water. Cool, and pour it onto the prepared orange. Serve with the duck.

When duck is done carve it and put in a hot serving dish; pour hot Cumberland sauce evenly over the duck and arrange watercress sprigs round this. Serves 4.

The fat that comes off the roasting duck is delicious and should be saved for use in other dishes. It is particularly good for roasting potatoes, to which the orange flavour gives a very special touch.

CUMBERLAND SAUCE

> 2 navel oranges
> juice of ½ lemon
> pinch of salt
> 1 teaspoon finely granulated sugar
> 2 teaspoons red-currant jelly
> ½ teaspoon mixed spice (ground cinnamon,
>   mace, and nutmeg)
> ⅓ cup port wine
> 1 teaspoon arrowroot

METHOD: Peel and squeeze the oranges. Grate the orange peel coarsely and put it into a pan with the squeezed juice (reserving 1 tablespoon juice), lemon juice, salt, sugar, jelly, and spice. Stir all together, heat gently, then bring to a boil. Remove from heat and add port; simmer for 5 minutes. Mix the arrowroot with the remaining orange juice; bring the sauce back to the boil and add the arrowroot. Stir until it thickens, and pour over the duck.

FRESH GARDEN PEAS

> 4 tablespoons butter
> 4 spring onions
> 4 lettuce leaves
> salt and pepper
> 1 lb. fresh garden peas, picked before they
>   are too large, shelled
> 1 sprig mint

METHOD: Put the butter in a pan over low heat and let it melt. Chop the spring onions and lettuce leaves and add to the butter with the seasoning. Pour the shelled peas over this, cover, and shake till all is simmering; simmer for 10 minutes. Do not add any water but shake from time to time. Put in a sprig of mint, drain, and serve. Serves 4.

This can have its full taste only if done with fresh peas. Frozen peas will be good but not as good.

MALAKOFF

> ¾ cup seedless raisins
> 2 tablespoons Kirsch
> 1 cup (½ lb.) unsalted butter
> 1¼ cups ground pistachio nuts
> 1¼ cups sugar
> ¼ cup heavy cream
> 12 ladyfingers, split

METHOD: Cut raisins in half and soak them in the Kirsch. Slightly warm the butter, beat it with a fork, add the ground pistachio nuts and the sugar. Beat all this for 5 minutes, until fluffy; stir in cream, raisins, and Kirsch.

Butter a 1½-quart charlotte mould and line the sides and bottom with the ladyfingers. Fill up with the butter mixture; cover the top with ladyfingers, press down well, and put in a cool place or chill for 24 hours. Turn out and serve with custard sauce (see index). Serves 6 to 8.

CUSTARD SAUCE

> 2 eggs
> 2 tablespoons sugar
> 1¼ cups milk
> 1 teaspoon vanilla extract
> 1 tablespoon brandy

METHOD: Beat eggs and sugar together in a bowl. Bring milk to a boil very slowly and pour it very slowly into the eggs, whisking well. Return the mixture to the pan and heat. Continue whisking until the custard thickens. Do not let it boil or it will curdle. Add flavouring and brandy after the custard is removed from the heat. Makes about 1½ cups.

It was anxious work to plan it all and to get everything ready at the same time. How glad I was of my long and thorough training and the discipline ingrained in me, of the experience in hotels, working at speed! And I had, as well, to keep a careful eye on those working under me and check them when necessary. [I know those little signs of disapproval.—R.G.]

We were a happy kitchen; though I was strict, I never drove my girls as Amy, that head housemaid, used to drive me, and they were eager and willing. I can see them now, in their crisp print dresses—blue for morning, pink for evening—and their clean white aprons. Evelyn, the kitchen-maid, was especially sensible and deft; she learned a great deal from me and could be trusted to do things in the way I liked, so that I could take my time off—and there was liberal free time—with a quiet mind.

This was one of the happiest and most fruitful times of my life, though it did not last long because there came the tug-of-war that besets most professional women, the choice between love and a home, and a career. Love won, and I married again. This time it was right, and in the family tradition, because my husband was in the Royal Navy. He says he married me for the way I make mint sauce, but we were, and are, very happy. While he was away at sea I took temporary posts, but only temporary, so that I could always be at home when he came back. Sometimes, though, his ship would be away for a tour of two years or more, so that I would spend months on end with the same family—as I did with that of Sir Anthony Eden in his London house.

As always, it is the kitchen at the Edens' I remember, a basement kitchen with lights on all the time. There was plenty of life, and we were all kept on our toes because only impeccable service was accepted. There was much entertaining, and I had glimpses of many notabilities. On a big dinner-party night things used really to hum because the butler and the pantry boy were at odds, but I and my kitchenmaid kept cool and collected, though often I used to "stew" inside.

For a small dinner I might make:

Oyster Soup

Saddle of Lamb

Champignons à la Crème

Fondue Niçoise

OYSTER SOUP

> 12 oysters in the shell—more if very small
> 1 whiting, cleaned, trimmed and cut in pieces
> 1 tablespoon chopped onion
> 1 tablespoon chopped celery
> salt and pepper
> a few peppercorns
> 6 cups fish stock or cold water
> 1 egg yolk
> 2 tablespoons milk

METHOD: Cover oysters with cold water, bring to the boil, and simmer until fully open (5 to 7 minutes). Beard them and simmer the beards, with the whiting, onion, celery, seasoning, and a few peppercorns, in the stock for 1 hour. Rub all through a sieve. Cut oysters into three or four pieces each; add these to the stock. Beat egg yolk with milk and add; stir over low heat until it thickens, but do not boil. Serve very hot. Serves 6 to 8.

ROAST SADDLE OF LAMB

> 1 5- to 6-lb. saddle of lamb
> ½ teaspoon salt
> ½ cup good clarified dripping from a meat
>   roast

METHOD: Preheat oven to 375°. Sprinkle the lamb with salt and cover with a well-buttered parchment paper or brown paper. Place the dripping in a roasting tin and melt it. Put the lamb into this and roast 15 minutes to the pound (4 pounds per hour). Baste every 10 to 15 minutes. About ½ hour before it is done, remove the paper so that the saddle may brown all over. Serves 5 to 6.

MY MINT SAUCE

> 4 heaping teaspoons very finely chopped fresh
>   mint
> salt to taste
> 2 teaspoons sugar
> 3 tablespoons wine vinegar

METHOD: Put the chopped mint into a small bowl and add the salt and sugar. Mix well, then mix in the wine vinegar; see that the consistency is nice and thick. Cover the bowl and let stand for at least 2 hours before serving in a sauceboat. Makes ¾ cup.

CHAMPIGNONS À LA CRÈME

½ lb. mushroom caps
4 tablespoons butter
½ teaspoon lemon juice
salt and pepper
⅔ cup cream
1 teaspoon chopped parsley

METHOD: Wipe the mushroom caps and put them into a pan with the butter, lemon juice, salt, and pepper, and cook, uncovered, over medium heat for 10 minutes. Spoon in the cream, stir well, and bring to the boil. Sprinkle the chopped parsley over the mushrooms and simmer for 2 or 3 minutes. Serve hot. Serves 4.

FONDUE NIÇOISE

3 tablespoons butter
1 tablespoon flour
⅝ cup milk
¾ cup grated Gruyère cheese
salt
pepper (4 turns of the grinder)
1 egg yolk
2 teaspoons white wine (if desired)
1 whole egg
breadcrumbs
butter
oil for frying

METHOD: Begin by making a roux: melt butter, add flour. Mix well over low heat and gradually add milk, stirring all the time. Add cheese and cook until the mixture "breathes" or bubbles. Season and remove from heat. Add egg yolk and stir well while adding white wine. Pour into a soup plate or shallow bowl and put in refrigerator to set, 20 minutes or more, depending on the coldness of the refrigerator.

Beat the egg well. Brown the breadcrumbs in butter and spread on waxed paper. Wet the hands with cold water and roll the fondue into balls the size of a plum. Dip each into beaten egg, then drop onto the breadcrumbs and roll it around until it is well coated. Heat a deep pan of oil until smoking hot (375°) and fry the fondue balls, six or eight at a time, for 5 to 7 minutes, until they are golden brown on the outside and runny inside. Drain well, keep hot, and serve with watercress. Serves 4 to 6.

More and more, though, I wanted to be at home. Home, in an East Sussex village, is the bungalow my father built and left to me. There our son was born and named Warwick in respectful tribute to the Countess; he was a sturdy fair-haired pickle of a child, and travels afield were over for a long time.

Now my husband has retired, so I no longer go out to service, though I still have that yearning to take a post in America.

For a time I worked odd evenings in and round the village, helping with dinner parties, going to people's rescue when they, or their cooks, were ill; then I worked at the White Hart until, as Rumer Godden has described, I ended up with her and now go in to Rye each afternoon and evening.

The rest of the time is taken in keeping the little bungalow shipshape, as my father would have said. It is full of family curiosities, mostly from far away, brought back by Grandfather, Father, and my husband from years at sea. Now Warwick is in the Royal Navy—he has just completed a long tour in the Far East, in HMS *Eagle*—and he too brings something each time he comes on leave.

These are my memories, but all through my cooking life there were what I call "characters and occasions." How odd some of those characters were! At the Castle there was one elderly lady who often came to luncheon with the Countess, though luncheon was hardly the right word; she was a vegetarian and would eat nothing but nuts. Her maid always came with her, and it was the maid who brought the nuts, all prepared, to me. Then there was the millionaire who, with all the lovely things made for his table, insisted that every sweet or pudding, and all the fruit, be covered with custard—and not my good homemade custard, but one made with a certain brand of custard powder. There was the baronet who wanted cooking lessons from me so that he could cook for his writer wife. He was so fired with the lessons that he bought himself a chef's hat and a set of knives; some dishes came out well, many were failures; and he became so downcast that in the end he settled for being the perfect butler and I was the chef. We were very happy together.

The "occasions" too will always stay in my mind. The afternoon when that same writer wife, Sheila Kaye-Smith, died: she just called to her husband from the head of the stairs that she did not feel well; he ran up to her and helped her down, and she died at the bottom. I helped him to carry her into the drawing room, where we laid her on the sofa. We could not believe she was dead. The house was bought by Rumer Godden and her husband, and Miss Godden has told how I came to go back there.

Then there was that early, early morning, in the soaking rain, when our doorbell rang and there was Miss Godden with her daughter, both ashen white under smoke and grime. The old house had been burned down in the night, and they had brought the two Pekingese to me to ask if I would take them in. These two scamps of Pekes have spent much of their time with me ever since.

BEING A COOK IS
NOT ALL COOKING

Being a cook is not all cooking. An upper servant is in a
position of trust and responsibility; she has to be discreet
with both those below and those above her and keep strict
control of her eyes, ears, and tongue—especially tongue.
Servants' halls, just as drawing rooms, are hotbeds of tittle-
tattle and gossip.

For a time I was cook at the country house of a German
couple. The lady—call her Baroness X—was young and very
much in awe of her far older husband, as we all were; he
looked the perfect pattern of a Prussian general and be-
haved like one, though he was a diplomat. His wife came
from a poor, much humbler family and—as her maid, Juliet,
told me—she used often to visit and help her mother with

money, though the Baron forbade her to do this. One morning it was announced that next day the Baron and Baroness were to go up to London for some grand dinner—it was rumoured, at the Palace; the Baron's chief had had unexpectedly to go to Berlin, and the Baron was to take his place. He was in high good humour, but the Baroness seemed strangely unhappy.

I met Juliet on the back stairs, bringing down the Baroness's gown. "*She* particularly wanted to go up to London today," said Juliet. "*He* won't let her." The master and mistress of the house were always "he" and "she." " '*Ach!* Nonsense! You will go up with me.' " It was the Baron's bullying way to a T.

Later on that morning the Baroness sent for me; she looked so pale and distraught that my heart ached for her and when she asked me if I would do something for her, "to give me great, great help," I could not refuse. "It must be someone I can trust," she said, and gave me my orders.

I caught the next train to London and took a taxi to the Baroness's bank, where I handed in a sealed envelope and waited. In return, another sealed envelope, but far bulkier, was handed to me; she had telephoned the manager to say that I was coming.

"Taxi all the way," the Baroness had said. "It will be quicker." So I took another taxi to a well-known jeweller in Oxford Street, where—my heart beating—I asked to see the manager. He took me into his office behind the shop, where I gave him a letter from the Baroness and then opened the bank envelope and counted out the notes, which came to a considerable sum. He took them, disappeared, and came back presently with a pearl necklace. The Baroness had given me a detailed description of it, and when I had made sure it was the right one, I did as she had told me and put it round my neck under my dress, though the thought of wearing anything so valuable made my knees weak and my mouth dry. Then I took a taxi to Cartier's, where I was ushered in by the commissionaire.

I had never been in such a shop and was almost overcome

by the expensive hush and glitter, the shining of the glass cases, and the elegance of the assistants; but I gave the Baroness's name—which they knew—and thankfully took off the pearls. The necklace, I said, was to be restrung and delivered without fail next day to the Park Lane house in time for the dinner.

That evening I was back in my kitchen. I had given my report to the Baroness and, though I could guess what lay behind my adventure, I had asked no questions; but as I turned to leave she had taken my hands and pressed them, with tears in her eyes. Poor young thing, I wonder what became of her.

The Baron tried me in many ways. He took an active part in the domestic arrangements, and soon after I came I was given a cook book marked with his favourite dishes, which I was to make—but the cook book was in German! I don't know how I managed, but I did.

One of the dishes he doted on was called Klops.

KLOPS

1 *lb. lean cooked pork*
2 *onions*
salt and pepper
6 *tablespoons butter*
3 *eggs, separated*
2 *teaspoons anchovy paste*
flour
2½ *cups meat stock or broth made with*
  2 *bouillon cubes*
1 *tablespoon chopped capers*

METHOD: Mince pork and onions together and season with salt and pepper. Melt butter and mix into the minced meat; add egg yolks and anchovy paste and mix well. Beat the egg whites until stiff but not dry and fold into the mixture. Bring to a boil some good stock in a shallow sauté pan; shape meat into balls (the size of a golf ball), roll in flour, and drop them into the boiling stock. Turn carefully and simmer about 10 minutes, then throw in the chopped capers. Serve Klops and remaining liquid in a serving dish.

Serve this with red cabbage cooked in boiling salt water with a clove for 10 minutes. Serves 4.

I never make it without thinking not of him but of the little Baroness.

Another summer I went with my temporary employer to Cowes, where she had a rented cottage for Cowes Week; the housemaid and parlourmaid came too, but what she wanted me down there for I scarcely knew, because she was hardly ever in, though now and again she would come back to the house with a gay and noisy party. She was a pretty woman, rich and amusing. The maids spoke of her as "Madam" with meaning: she had, as they soon told me, a "friend," a naval commander, who, they assured me, had taken the cottage for her. He liked to come quietly for one of my dinners—"dinner for *two*!" as the parlourmaid said— but when the regatta was on I suppose Madam found those tête-à-têtes dull.

One evening she told me she was going to a cocktail party but would be back for dinner with the Commander. He arrived but she did not; after waiting impatiently he decided to fetch her. I kept the dinner hot, but the hours went by with no sign, no telephone call. Finally I sent the maids to bed and, at midnight, went to bed myself.

Next morning I woke very early, before the maids were up, and came downstairs. All the lights were on in the hall, looking odd blazing away in the morning sunshine. In the drawing room, which was lit up too, the telephone was on the floor, a chair was overturned, and the floor was strewn with jewellery—Madam's diamonds, as I recognized. I hastily went over the floor, scooping diamonds up into my pocket, turned off the lights, and put the room to rights before the maids came down. They asked what time "she" had come in. I said it was before I went to bed but told them nothing of what was in my pocket.

I waited for the bell to ring, because Madam always rang

when she wanted her breakfast. At last it rang, and I went quickly up before either of the girls could answer it, knocked at the door, and went in. Madam was sitting up in bed, looking pale and ill and holding her head; when she took her hand down I saw she had the most beautiful black eye.

I thought it better not to remark on it so I asked if she would like some coffee, but she groaned and said she felt too awful. Then—and I don't know what made me think of it—I suggested a bottle of Bass from the refrigerator. "Mrs. Manders, you're a bloody good pal," she said, and I fetched up a bottle and a glass. Then I quietly took the jewellery out of my pocket and asked her to check it. Not a word more was said by either of us, but "He must have been a proper naval chap," was my husband's comment when I told him.

The chief thing I remember cooking that week in Cowes was the bread I made for the house. The maids said it was delicious and used to coax me to make it and, as I had plenty of time, we had fresh bread every day.

BROWN BREAD

2½ cups whole-wheat flour
1½ cups white flour
1 tablespoon salt
3 tablespoons sugar
1½ teaspoons baking soda
2 eggs, slightly beaten
2 cups buttermilk

METHOD: Preheat oven to 350°. Sift together all dry ingredients, add slightly beaten eggs, and stir. Add buttermilk and mix well. Put batter into a large oiled loaf pan, about 10 by 5 inches, and bake for 55 minutes.

You can't buy bread like that from a baker.

After the week, Madam decided to go on the Hay diet. What a nuisance that was—everything cooked in a Haybox; vegetables and fruit not to be eaten at the same meal; no starch, which meant no bread. We had had a fortnight

of this when one morning she came into the kitchen.
"What's that lovely smell?"

I was just taking the bread out of the oven, two loaves,
crisp and fresh and warm. "Smells bloody good," said
Madam.

I had had more than enough of the Hay diet, so without
saying anything I cut off a crust, spread it with butter, and
put it on a plate. She looked at it for a moment, her eyes
glistening like a child's—what a pretty woman she was!
Then she said, "To hell with the bloody diet." In the end
she ate half a loaf.

IN THE KITCHEN

A kitchen need not be elaborate; in fact it is surprising how few gadgets and few utensils a good chef has. These are, to me, the essentials of a good working kitchen:

> Six assorted wooden spoons
> Two spatulas (of which one should be metal)
> A set of sharp knives, kept separately, with corks
>   to protect their tips; these should be wiped,
>   not washed
> Bread and poultry cutter
> Two tablespoons
> Two dessert spoons
> Two teaspoons
> Two strong forks

One soup ladle
One fish slicer
One egg slicer
Egg beater or electric mixer with mincer
  appliance
One whisk
One pair of kitchen scissors
One tin opener
Steel tongs
One steak beater
One flour sprinkler
One cheese grater
One conical gravy strainer
One pastry bag and rosettes
One garlic squeezer
One lemon squeezer
Salt and pepper grinders
Fine sieves with handles: one large, one medium,
  and one small
One cake rack
One set cake tins
One flan case
Pastry board and rolling pin
Pastry and cocktail cutters
One set dariole moulds (pastry moulds)
Soufflé dishes: one large, one medium
Covered casserole dishes
One double boiler
One steam cooker
Six assorted saucepans
One omelette pan
Frying pans: one large, one small
One deep-frying pan and basket
One large fish kettle
Two baking tins
One Yorkshire pudding tin
Mixing bowls: two large, one small
Assorted heatproof pudding basins
Standard measuring cup or jug
Kitchen scales and accurate weights

One vegetable grater
Foil and greaseproof paper
Pudding cloths
Chopping boards, one for onions only

This may seem a formidable list, but add up what is in most kitchens, and by contrast it will seem quite modest.

I always like to have parsley standing ready in water on the kitchen window sill, and have, too, a small herb patch very near my kitchen so that I do not have to trudge to the vegetable garden; parsley, lemon thyme, mint, tarragon, sage are all easy to grow; the rest of my herbs I buy dried and keep in bottles in a dark place.

In the larder I keep, if possible, small bottles of Kirsch, Curaçao, and brandy; these last me a long time. There should also be cooking sherry and "ends" of red and white wine. If a white wine is bought especially for cooking, an inexpensive dry Spanish Graves is quite satisfactory.

I never find it necessary to buy bones for soup, as I keep everything in the way of bones or carcasses that comes from the table; I pick the carcasses clean of meat. A nourishing soup can be made from things most people throw away: cold vegetables, odds and ends of sauces, bacon rinds, lettuce leaves, sour cream; and, though I say it myself, my soups are delicious.

There is as much planning as doing in cooking. I make it my rule to know first how many there will be at table, as nothing is more maddening for a cook than to be told when everything is ready, "There will be one or two extra." I find it hard to keep my temper then. Also one must be warned if the meal may be kept waiting, as certain things, such as soufflés, cannot wait. [With us the rules have become horridly upset. Poor Mrs. Manders may suddenly be told there will be one more for dinner; timing is impossible, as often I am "caught up" into work, and when I do come down we sometimes plead for another ten minutes. I don't know how Mrs. Manders bears it, but she does. We have had to cut out soufflés except on party nights.—R.G.]

If there is to be a cold sweet on any menu, I make it the day before, as I do all batters; for oxtail soup or stew I need three days' warning; for my steak and kidney pie or pudding I need two. When I have a new recipe I sit down quietly and study it, size it up, and consider whether it promises well; then I make sure I have everything it requires and go about it in a normal way. If it doesn't turn out well the first time, I have learned not to blame the recipe but to see what *I* did wrong. (Miss Godden says, "Where's your halo?" but this is true!)

Of course I have made mistakes, some of them bad ones. The first time I was asked to serve grilled soles I cleaned them carefully but left the heads on; when they were taken to the dining room they looked perfect except for the eyes, which glared viciously. I had no time to take the heads off them, and my employer and her guests were not amused. On another occasion, when I was employed by a bachelor gentleman who was very, very critical, I decided to make a lemon soufflé for his dinner sweet. When it was put into its silver serving dish, with whipped cream piped over it, I thought it looked grand, but a few minutes later the butler came back, carrying the broken masterpiece, and said in a grave voice, "Your master sends his compliments but he does not require a spare tire for his car." Imagine my horror. I had used double the amount of gelatine.

To avoid such mistakes and to be able to concentrate, I try to keep the kitchen quiet and orderly. I do not let utensils pile up. If I cannot wash pans at once I put them to soak; I do not like to talk while I am working [Oh, Mrs. Manders! When did I hear all your stories?—R.G.]; and I *cannot* have children in the kitchen, it is too great a responsibility.

In my years of service in big houses where there were well-trained staffs, I picked up many hints about caring for household things from, for instance, the housemaids, and for clothes from the ladies' maids and valets. Some of these out-of-the-way hints are the following.

THE CARE OF HANDS

After peeling onions, a little dried mustard rubbed well into your hands will remove all trace of smell.

To keep hands from getting rough and stained, wash the hands in warm water; rub them over with a little light oil—almond, for instance. Now take as much granulated sugar as will go on a sixpence and rub it into the hands, especially fingers or thumbs where dirt is ingrained. Wash off in warm water and finish by rubbing in lotion; Johnson's Baby lotion is splendid. This treatment leaves the hands smooth and white; it was especially useful to ladies' maids, who, though they had to wash underclothes and clean shoes, needed to keep their hands nice.

TO REMOVE FLY MARKS ON SILK SHADES OR CURTAINS

Dust the stained silk or the parts that are "fly-soiled" with finely powdered French chalk. Mix together very well 1½ ounces soft soap, 5 ounces methylated spirit (denatured alcohol), and 5 ounces water. Rub this mixture carefully and lightly on the stains, on both sides of the fabric, using a soft rag or sponge. Wash the parts treated with lukewarm water and press gently with an iron, not too hot.

USES FOR TEA LEAVES

Keep used tea leaves. Place them in a basin of water and soak them for ½ hour. Stir and use instead of soap and water to clean varnished paint surfaces.

Pour boiling water on used tea leaves and leave for 1 hour; the liquid can then be used to clean mirrors, windows, glasses, varnished doors, furniture, linoleum, and muddy black suede shoes.

TO CLEAN GLASS

To clean cut-glass decanters or vases, tear up newspaper into small pieces; drop these into decanter, add cold water, and fill up alternately with small pieces of paper and water till it is nearly full. Shake well from time to time; leave overnight. Resume shaking; remove paper and wash out until clear of all paper. Wash glass in warm soapy water, using a small brush to get into intricate parts. Rinse in cold water containing a little vinegar. Dry with fluffless linen cloth, then rub with soft tissue paper. To induce a high polish, brush with a little French chalk.

To make glass sparkle, add a little bluing to the water; but the best polisher for glass, especially a lens, and for silver, is what my mother used to call "lady's breath": breathe on the surface until it is steamed over, and then rub up until there is a real shine (not very hygienic but wonderfully effective).

TO CLEAN BROWN LEATHER SHOES

Rub well with the inside skin of a banana. Do this each morning and let dry, then polish with a soft piece of rag. Afterwards use a good brown shoe cream. A little care, and the shoes will always look like new.

TO CLEAN WOOL DRESSES, CARPETS

All sorts of woollen things can be cleaned with potato water, without injury to their colour. Put 2½ cups of water in a bowl and grate into it two raw potatoes. Strain through a sieve into a larger bowl containing 2½ more cups of water. Let this settle, then strain off the clear part into bottles for future use.

Dip a sponge into the liquid. With it, rub the soiled articles carefully, then wash with clean cold water.

TO CLEAN JEWELLERY

Apply camphorated chalk (most chemists stock it) with a soft old toothbrush. Brush chalk off and polish with a piece of plush or velvet. Gold, silver, or any trinkets may be treated this way with excellent results. For gold, the best cleanser is jeweller's rouge, which you can buy from a good jeweller. Rub on with a soft damp cloth. When dry, brush off with a soft brush or silver-brush.

TO MAKE ROSE POT-POURRI

Gather lemon verbena leaves, geranium, rose, and lavender blossoms. Pull off the petals and dry them thoroughly and slowly (not in the sun). Put rose petals in the bottom of a jar and sprinkle with salt. Add half the dried lavender and whatever other petals you have found; put in a few cracked cloves and some small pieces of cinnamon stick, and sprinkle with salt. Now add some more rose petals and repeat the process.

When jar is full, put in a few drops of eau de Cologne and two ounces of powdered orris root. Cover the jar for a few weeks. Be sure the leaves are perfectly dry; if not, the mixture will not keep. Stir well from time to time.

PARTIES

I love the feeling of a house when there is going
to be a party: the bustle and expectation; the planning of
the menu and the table and flowers; the getting out of
china and glass. It gives a new thrill to the usual domestic
round and conjures up the resources of the house; and I
love the cooking, though it is hard work, as I like to do it
all myself—with someone to act as kitchenmaid if possible.
[Usually me.—R.G.] I am against getting in a caterer's staff.

Having lived so long in India, Rumer Godden likes to
give a curry luncheon—not too often, because my curry
really is a marathon, there are so many complementary
dishes to make. Miss Godden has a beautiful Bengali friend,
the musician Rajeshwari Dutta, who gave us the recipe for

Bengal Curry (see index), but I prefer my Malayan Curry; I was once in Sussex with a theatrical family who had a Malayan house guest, and she taught me the Malayan way.

MALAYAN CURRY

> 4 lbs. boneless lamb (from leg or shoulder)
> 2½ tablespoons vegetable oil
> 2 onions, chopped
> 4 cloves garlic, crushed
> salt and pepper
> 1¼ cups stock, preferably chicken

METHOD: Cut up raw lamb into chunky pieces, discarding excess fat. Heat oil in a large pan and put in the chopped onion, garlic, and meat. Season. Reduce heat and cook, stirring for at least 10 minutes; do not let it brown. Add stock and set pan to one side to keep warm.

Now make the curry sauce:

> 1¼ tablespoons mildly hot curry powder
> 2 teaspoons flour
> 1¼ teaspoons ground ginger
> 1 tablespoon ground cinnamon
> 1¼ teaspoons turmeric
> ⅔ cup chicken stock
> ¼ cup fresh grated coconut
> 1 tablespoon finely crushed and pounded chili peppers
> 2 tablespoons pounded coriander seeds
> 1 tablespoon fresh lemon grass, or dried lemon verbena

METHOD: Mix curry powder, flour, ginger, cinnamon, and turmeric into a smooth paste, using some of the chicken stock; now add the rest of the ingredients and add to the meat, garlic, and onion mixture. Mix well together and simmer, covered, about 1 to 1½ hours, or until meat is tender. Serves 8.

The side dishes, or "toli molies," take the longest time to prepare, so I will give these in detail. First:

SAFFRON RICE

> 1 tablespoon salt
> 2 cups Patna rice *
> ¼ teaspoon powdered saffron
> ½ cup seedless raisins

METHOD: Bring 2 quarts salted water to a boil and add the rice. After rice has boiled for 5 minutes, stir in the saffron with a fork. Cook the rice until tender and drop in the raisins. Let these swell a minute or two, then drain the rice. Steam over boiling water to separate the grains. Put in a serving dish and decorate the top with some of the crisp fried onions. Send to table with the meat and side dishes. Serves 8.

CURRIED PRAWNS †

> boiling water
> salt
> ½ cucumber, peeled, diced, seeds removed
> 4 teaspoons grated coconut
> ¼ cup chopped onions or shallots
> 1 clove garlic, very finely chopped
> ¼ cup butter
> 2 teaspoons flour
> 1¼ teaspoons ground turmeric
> 1¼ teaspoons ground cinnamon
> 1¼ teaspoons ground cloves
> 2 teaspoons thinly sliced green ginger
> ½ teaspoon sugar
> 1¼ teaspoons salt
> ⅔ cups stock from cooked prawns
> 24 fresh or frozen prawns, cooked and shelled
> 1¼ teaspoons lemon juice

* May be obtained in many specialty grocery stores. Carolina long-grain rice may be substituted.
† Large shrimp.

METHOD: Put into a pan of salted boiling water the prepared cucumber and cook gently about 2 minutes or until nearly tender. Remove from heat and drain well. Pour ⅔ cup boiling water over grated coconut. Let it stand 20 minutes, then strain off liquid. Cover coconut again with ⅔ cup boiling water. Let stand ½ hour, then strain through fine muslin, squeezing it well.

Sauté onions and garlic lightly in butter, add the flour, turmeric, cinnamon, cloves, ginger, sugar, and 1¼ teaspoons salt. Stir in the stock. Cook covered, slowly 15 minutes. Now add the prawns and cucumber. Cover closely and keep in a warm place for ½ hour so that the dish may blend thoroughly. Reheat, add coconut and lemon juice, bring to a boil, and serve. Serves 8.

CRISP FRIED ONIONS

4 large onions
flour
oil for frying

Peel onions and cut them into very thin rings crosswise. Roll them in flour and fry, a few at a time, in deep oil at 375°. When they are just beginning to colour, in about 5 or 10 minutes, remove and drain. Keep hot. Serves 8.

OTHER CURRY ACCOMPANIMENTS

Have ready some small saucer-sized dishes for the following:

Tomatoes: Skin and cut into thin slices, sprinkle with chopped parsley.

Hard-cooked eggs: Slice thin.

Chopped parsley.

Chutney, homemade (see index).

Mangoes: I buy a tin of these and slice them.

Potatoes, cold, boiled, and diced, with lemon juice sprinkled on them and a few thin slices of lemon peel.

Grated coconut, which must be lightly browned in a warm oven (300°) for 10 to 15 minutes.

Cucumber, peeled and sliced.

Fresh peanuts or monkey nuts: Shell, remove skins, and brown lightly in oven with the coconut.

Hot pickle sauce, such as Ranji's, which contains chili pepper.

Prawn crackers, bought in a tin. Warm through.

Poppadums: Thin wafers of grain and spices available at specialty food shops. Allow one at least per person. Have ready a deep pan with smoking oil (375°). Put poppadums in one by one; as they start to rise and curl, flatten them with a spatula. Remove as soon as they turn golden, and drain well. Put into a large dish and keep very hot.

DHÁL SAUCE

1 cup dried lentils *
1 large onion
4 tablespoons butter
boiling water or stock (at least 2½ cups)
salt and pepper
1¼ teaspoon turmeric

METHOD: Soak lentils overnight. Slice onion thin. Melt 2 tablespoons butter in a medium-size saucepan and sauté the onion until golden. Remove from heat and pour in boiling stock. Add lentils, season, cover, and return to heat. Bring to boil and simmer until the lentils become soft. Then stir with a wooden spoon until sauce becomes a thick paste. Add turmeric. Keep stirring to prevent burning. (If a double boiler is used, it eliminates some of the need to stir.) Add 2 tablespoons butter and keep hot until serving time. Serves 8.

This completes the curry luncheon.

For a curry luncheon I serve no first course, as when the guests come in the curry must be on the table, which is set

* Dhál grain is difficult to obtain, so I use ordinary lentils.

without a centrepiece. There is, in fact, no room for flowers, nor are they needed, because the table looks so colourful and pretty. The curry itself is in the centre, bubbling gently in a chafing dish over a flame, and around it, in a circle of small dishes and bowls, are the "complements" in all their colours: the golden-brown coconut, pale green cucumber, gold mangoes, browned nuts, prawns in curry sauce, potato with lemon, prawn crackers, and so forth. I bring in two big bowls of rice and set them at either end of the table; in one the rice is plain, in the other it is saffron; both are strewn with crisp fried onions. There are sauceboats of dhál, which should accompany curry, and when everyone is seated and served I hand round hot poppadums, those thin, crisp, crackling chupatti-biscuits.

After a curry it is wise to have only cooling fruit and cream, so I often serve Macédoine of Melon.

MACÉDOINE OF MELON

1 honeydew melon
2½ tablespoons lemon juice
2 or 3 eating apples
2 or 3 dessert pears
2 navel oranges
¼ lb. black or white grapes
2 fresh peaches
a few pineapple slices, tinned or fresh
2½ teaspoons finely granulated sugar
2½ teaspoons Kirsch or Maraschino
1 cup strawberries, fresh or frozen
6 Maraschino cherries

METHOD: Cut top off melon, and see that it stands straight on the serving platter. Remove carefully all flesh from top and cut into nice chunks, not too large. Now remove seeds from the melon itself, using a spoon, and take away the flesh, being careful not to go too near the skin, otherwise it may leak. Cut this up the way the flesh from the lid was done. Put all into a large mixing bowl.

Skin and core the apples, quarter, and chop up in pieces, sprinkle with lemon juice; do the same with the pears and

oranges, removing *all* pith and skins from the orange segments. Skin and seed the grapes; try to keep these nearly
whole. Skin peaches and slice. Chop pineapple slices. Add all
this fruit to the melon chunks, sprinkle with sugar, add Kirsch
or Maraschino; mix all together very lightly and thoroughly.

Hull the strawberries and place these gently in the mixture
of fruit. Now put it into the empty melon and put on the lid.
Keep in refrigerator until wanted. Before presenting your
melon, place the Maraschino cherries on top of the fruit,
replace lid, and serve with cream. Serves 8.

Buffet parties with us seem to fall into two patterns, one
for the younger generation, the other for the older people,
who have perhaps a finer taste in food. "Don't give the boys
and girls your pomponettes," says Miss Godden. "They
haven't the palate." So I plan for them quite differently.
Again we have a central dish, perhaps a paella, for which I
prepare everything in the morning.

PAELLA

1 4-to-5-lb. stewing chicken, cut up
salt and 4 peppercorns
16 or 18 crayfish tails, if available *
24 fresh mussels or cherrystone clams, or
    frozen or canned equivalent
1 green pepper
3 canned pimientos
½ lb. cooked ham
1½ lbs. fresh or frozen prawns (large shrimp)
1 lb. fresh, or 1 10-oz. package frozen, peas
½ cup cooking oil
2 fairly large onions, chopped
2 cloves garlic, crushed
2 cups long-grained rice (Spanish, if available)
4 to 5 cups chicken stock
salt and pepper
½ teaspoon saffron

* Crayfish are found on the Pacific Coast, around New Orleans, and in
some other southern areas of the United States. You may omit them, or
substitute cooked lobster or crabmeat.

METHOD: Put chicken in pot with water to cover and bring to a boil. Turn down heat and simmer uncovered 1½ to 2 hours or until meat is tender. Add ¾ teaspoon salt and 4 peppercorns after first hour.

While chicken is cooking, defrost and drain all frozen products except shrimp and peas. Boil the crayfish tails in salted water for 8 minutes; drain and cut into 1-inch pieces, leaving shells on. Scrub fresh mussels or clams in three or four changes of water. Steam in covered kettle containing 1 cup boiling salted water over high heat; the shells will open in 3 to 4 minutes; discard any that don't. Remove shells; drain shellfish and set aside. Remove seeds and white part from green pepper; slice pepper and pimientos into strips.

Cut ham into ¾-inch cubes. (*Chorizos,* little Spanish sausages, may be used instead; sauté to get rid of fat.) Boil shrimp in salted water 3 minutes; shell and devein. Boil peas in salted water, but undercook; drain and keep warm.

When the chicken is done, take pieces out of the pot and drain on a plate. Strain and reserve the stock. Remove skin and bones, break meat into pieces, and slice breast into thick fingers. Set aside all but choice meat for another purpose.

The reason for having all these things done and ready is that the paella must be assembled and cooked rather quickly, and it must be watched until completion. Preheat oven to 325°. Heat the oil in a large paella pan or wide flameproof casserole, capacity about 6 quarts (a copper preserving kettle is ideal). Add onions and garlic and stir around a minute or two. Add rice and stir over low heat until golden, about 5 minutes. Pour in 4 cups chicken stock, add 2½ teaspoons salt and ¼ teaspoon pepper, bring to a boil, then add saffron. Lower heat and stir frequently until rice softens, about 10 minutes. Put in chicken, crayfish, and ham. Mix gently with a fork until all are thoroughly warmed, about 5 minutes. If stock seems all absorbed at this point, add a little more. Remove from stove, add mussels or clams, and place spoonfuls of peas and shrimp round the top of the dish. Cover with lid or foil and put in preheated 325° oven for 10 to 15 minutes. Rice should be dry and fluffy. Before serving, decorate with pimiento and green-pepper strips. Serves 12.

Round this I set out savoury finger food: sausages on toothpicks, cheese éclairs, prawn sticks, dainty open sandwiches.

CHEESE ÉCLAIRS

> 4 tablespoons butter
> ⅔ cup sifted all-purpose flour
> 3 eggs

METHOD: Preheat oven to 425°. Put ⅔ cup water into a heavy pan, add butter; bring *just* to a boil and remove from heat. Add flour, stir vigorously, add one egg, and stir like mad until well blended. Follow the same procedure with the other eggs. Cool. Grease a baking sheet. Put batter in a pastry bag and pipe in 24 2-inch lengths onto sheet. Bake for 20 minutes. Cool, slit each éclair up the side, and fill with Mornay Sauce.

MORNAY SAUCE

> 2 tablespoons butter
> 2 tablespoons flour
> 2½ tablespoons grated Parmesan cheese
> ¾ cup milk
> salt
> Cayenne pepper
> 1 egg yolk
> ¼ cup finely diced smoked cheese

METHOD: Melt butter in a heavy pan, stir in flour and grated cheese, then gradually add the milk, stirring all the time. Cook until thick, remove from heat, season, and beat in egg yolk. Cool and add the smoked cheese. Makes about 1 cup.

Any flaked cold cooked fish such as salmon may be used instead of the smoked cheese.

With the paella a wine can be served that would not ordinarily be good enough for a dinner party. A Spanish Burgundy goes well with the mussels and other shellfish.

After this I serve Soufflé Citron, one of my favourite sweets.

SOUFFLÉ CITRON

> 6 white peaches (tinned)
> ⅓ cup brandy
> 4 lemons
> 4 eggs, separated
> ¾ cup finely granulated sugar
> pinch of salt
> 1 teaspoon Maraschino
> 1 tablespoon gelatine
> 1¼ cups cream
> sweetened marron purée

METHOD: Drain the peaches and soak in the brandy overnight. Grate lemon rinds finely. Squeeze lemon juice and strain it. Put egg yolks into a bowl with the sugar and salt. With a wooden spoon, beat vigorously for 10 minutes. Add the grated lemon rind and the strained juice, continue beating until well blended, and add a little Maraschino. Heat gelatine in 2½ tablespoons water, stirring, until all is dissolved. Beat egg whites until very stiff. Pour gelatine over lemon-juice mixture, stir well, then fold in whites. Pour into a silver entrée dish or glass bowl and put into refrigerator to set. When set, remove from refrigerator.

Whip the cream until thick but not "buttery"; attach a large rosette shape to pastry bag and pour in the whipped cream. Pipe a large rosette in centre of the soufflé, then decorate the edges with smaller patterns. Drain the peaches again, cut each one in pieces, and arrange, petal-like, around the centre rosette; the surplus can be arranged round the piped edge. Finally, fill pastry bag with marron purée and squeeze it into curls in the spaces on the soufflé; make one large curl on top of the centre rosette. Rechill. Serve with sugar wafers. Serves 6.

We use a coloured breakfast cloth for these "young parties"; it looks gay, and wine spills on it are no great matter.

The dining room at Hartshorn House is white and gold, so a rough-spun cloth in shades of gold and turquoise looks well, as does a deep purple and pink one that seems to ask for anemones in bowls. I remember Monsieur Jean Renoir telling me that in Mexico a tablecloth like this is simply called "the colour": for these parties it certainly needs no other description. I find that young people immensely appreciate a really pretty table.

But the nights I really enjoy are for the more sophisticated, for the gourmets—not gourmands or greedies, but those that appreciate fine cooking. I remember a June party, a buffet for twenty-four, where the cloth was white, embroidered with white roses, and we had real white roses to match. The cut glass glittered, and the silver shone in the way I like to see.

We served soup first from a trolley—Consommé Julienne with wine. It would have been iced if the night had been hot; however, it was chilly and so I served the soup hot with diced cucumber and slivers of lemon peel.

CONSOMMÉ JULIENNE WITH WINE

> ½ lb. shin of beef
> 1 onion or leek, sliced
> 1 carrot, sliced
> 1 stalk celery, sliced
> 1 chili pepper
> a few peppercorns
> 1 eggshell
> 1 egg white
> ⅓ cup sherry
> 1 carrot, cut into thin strips

METHOD: Cut beef into small pieces, remove all fat, put into a stew pan, and add 6 cups cold water. Bring slowly to the boil; skim well. Put in the vegetables. Tie the peppercorns and the chili pepper together in a muslin or cheesecloth bag. Simmer 5 or 6 hours with the lid off. Strain through cheesecloth. Allow to cool.

Crush an eggshell into small pieces. Beat the egg white slightly and mix with the shell. Stir this into the soup. Bring to a boil, stirring well, and then boil for 3 minutes without stirring. Add sherry and strain through two thicknesses of cheesecloth. Serves 6.

This is the foundation of most consommés. Consommé Julienne is garnished with thin strips of carrot.

Then the guests came to the table, which was set out with chicken and asparagus horns, salmon mousse (see index), pâté en gelée, fresh Russian salad, green salad Niçoise (for this, lettuce must be shredded, as otherwise it is awkward to eat at a buffet).

CHICKEN AND ASPARAGUS HORNS

1 recipe puff pastry (see index)
1 egg, beaten
2 tablespoons gelatine
5 cups chicken stock
3 8-oz. jars boned cooked chicken breasts
2½ tablespoons white wine
salt and pepper
2½ tablespoons cream
32 cooked or tinned asparagus tips

METHOD: For this you will need horn-shaped metal moulds around which to wind the pastry. Preheat oven to 425°. Roll out pastry in long thin strips 1 inch wide; wind these round horn shapes. Cut and seal edges by brushing with a pastry brush dipped in beaten egg and pressing edges together. Grease a baking sheet, arrange horns on it, brush them with beaten egg, and put in oven for 10 to 15 minutes or until they are brown. Remove and slide the pastry carefully from the shapes. Cool on wire racks.

Soften gelatine in ½ cup chicken stock. Cut chicken breasts into 1-inch slices. Heat remaining chicken stock, add softened gelatine, and stir until dissolved. Add white wine, a little salt and pepper, and the cream. Stir and put in refrigerator until the aspic has *just* begun to set, about 20 minutes. Remove from the refrigerator and stir; it should be about the consistency of unbeaten egg white. Dip pieces of chicken breast in this, put them into horns, fold the asparagus tips, and insert them so that they just peep out of the horns. If the horns look as though they need more sauce, add some carefully, but do not hide the asparagus tips. Chill until aspic is set. Arrange daintily on an entrée dish and sprinkle with watercress or parsley. Makes about 32 horns.

PÂTÉ EN GELÉE

> 1 *tablespoon gelatine*
> 2 *10½-oz. cans beef consommé*
> 3 *ozs. cream cheese*
> 4 *tablespoons pâté de foie gras (an inexpensive*
>   *kind will do)*
> *salt*
> *pepper*
> *onion salt*
> *lettuce leaves for garnish*

METHOD: Stir half the gelatine in half the consommé over medium heat until the gelatine dissolves. Pour into the bottom of a mould and chill until it sets. Mix cheese and pâté until they are well creamed together. Add seasonings to taste, and spread the mixture on top of the jellied consommé. Melt remaining gelatine in the rest of the consommé and pour over the pâté. The layers of jellied consommé should be about ¾ inch thick; the cream cheese and pâté, about ½ inch thick. Chill until set and turn out on a dish of fresh young lettuce leaves. Serves 8.

This was given to me by an American friend of Miss Godden's, Mrs. H. H. Pike of New York.

For fingers that might get a little greasy, there was a bowl of warm water in which I floated lavender and rose petals.

The crown of the evening was a new "creation": that is the right description. I called it "Fraises à la Rumer." *

* I felt a little embarrassed at having such a confection called after me, but Mrs. Manders loves really to "go to town" when there is any kind of party. I always felt it would be a wonderful thing to have a rose called after me, but perhaps this—dare I call it a pudding?—is better.—R.G.

FRAISES À LA RUMER

> 6 egg whites
> pinch of salt
> 1½ cups finely granulated sugar
> 2 quarts strawberries
> 2 tablespoons Kirsch
> 2½ cups heavy cream

METHOD: The meringue should be made 24 hours in advance. Grease three large baking sheets. Preheat oven to 475°. Beat egg whites with salt and ¼ cup sugar until stiff. Add the remaining sugar and continue beating until the mixture stands up in peaks. Put this into a large pastry bag and form a solid flat circle 9 inches in diameter on one of the prepared baking sheets. Next, make another circle 7 inches in diameter, another one of 5 inches, and lastly one of 3 inches. Put these into the oven, turn off heat, and leave for 8 hours. Remove, and when they are quite cool place each one very carefully on a clean working area.

Hull the strawberries, except for the largest one, which is reserved for the final touch. Put the fruit into a large bowl and sprinkle over it a little Kirsch; be careful not to use too much. While the strawberries are lying in the bowl with the liqueur, whip the cream until firm but not buttery. Insert a large rosette funnel into the pastry bag and fill it with the whipped cream.

Now put the largest meringue onto a circular platter (preferably silver) larger than 9 inches. Arrange strawberries on this, covering it completely, and pipe cream over them. Follow this procedure with the 7-inch and then the 5-inch meringue. Finally put the 3-inch meringue on top; pipe the remaining cream onto it in large rosettes, then put on this as a crowning the single large unhulled strawberry. The whole sweet should now look like a wedding cake. Serves 20.

When the table was cleared and reset with the gilt and turquoise dessert plates, I carried the strawberry tower in and could not help feeling pleased when there was applause. The *fraises* were served with petits fours.

Then there was Irish coffee.

IRISH COFFEE

> 1 *pint freshly made coffee*
> 3 *tablespoons Irish whisky, heated but not*
>   *boiling*
> 3 *tablespoons heavy cream*

Pour the coffee into a heated coffee pot or jug, pour in the whisky, and, lastly, pour in the cream, over *the back* of a tablespoon. Serve immediately. Serves 8.

Miss Godden says I make it all sound too splendid. Well, it was splendid but not at all splendiferous; everything was homemade and we did it all ourselves, she, her husband, the excellent daily "help," and I. I say it turned out well because of the love and care put into it. Each party becomes a happy memory: there was one, a tea, for the wives of the artisans who worked on the house; there was a dinner for Miss Godden's mother on her ninetieth birthday, and there are dents in the dining-room ceiling made by exploding champagne corks to mark the happiness of that event (and the exuberance of Miss Godden's husband). There were christenings for the grandchildren, and Christmas feasts. Each occasion was a success, and I felt proud. "You ought to be proud," Miss Godden has said. "You made many people happy and content. Come to that," she added, "you have been making people happy and content most of your life. Not many can say that."

Miss Godden listens politely to all I say; her husband says I never use two words if nineteen will do. (Anyone who reads this book will know he is wrong.) But indeed, when I look back on that clumsy little Olga—known as Mary— under the thumb of the ogre Amy, yet taking her first steps into her chosen life, I cannot find words to tell how miraculous it seems to me in the way it has all turned out. I can only say I am grateful and most happy and content—but I still want to go to America.

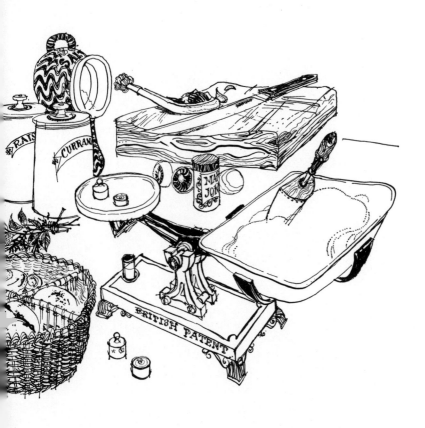

Part Two/Recipes

A NOTE BY
RUMER GOODEN

These are some of Mrs. Manders' "lovely dishes."
Of course she does not serve one of these every night, but
we decided she should not include in this book such things
as plain roasts, pies, or grills; she says anyone who can cook
at all must know how to cook these. As a matter of fact,
grills are not her strong point; perhaps, after that hotel
work with its "traffic," she has an aversion to them.

Using up leftovers is an art in itself, but except for one
or two special recipes we have not gone into it here. Like
most excellent cooks, Mrs. Manders cooks largely by instinct and by eye, so that it is difficult for her to work out
any recipe in precise terms. "Put in some butter," she says,
"a little flour . . . a cupful of rice . . . a wineglass of
sherry . . . bake in a moderate oven." "Yes, Mrs. Manders,
but one must be exact. *How* much butter? *How much* is
'a little'? *What* sort of cup? Wineglass? *What* tempera-

ture?" A pitying look comes on her face; then, when she sees I really mean I must know, a tormented look succeeds it, but gradually I elicit that "some butter" is usually an ounce; "a little" is a tablespoonful; a "cup" is a teacup. "And a wineglass of sherry?" "A sherry glass, of course," she says, exasperated. A moderate oven is 350° Fahrenheit; a hot one, 400°; very hot, 450°.

While we have tried to translate these terms into precise directions, Mrs. Manders is right: cooking is not and never can be an exact science. Timing and temperatures have to be adapted to circumstances: a roast that comes from the butcher on a warm day—or has been in a warm kitchen—and goes almost straight into the oven will need less cooking time than a roast the same weight that has been kept in the refrigerator until the last moment. Some apples are sweeter than others and so need less sugar; herbs taste stronger when they are fresh, and so on. Mrs. Manders says cooks rely far too much on the printed word, instead of cultivating an instinct. "You have to use your common sense *and* your imagination," she says. "Tell yourself, 'I'll add this—or that—just to see.' That, after all, is how most the famous dishes were made."

Her *bouquet garni* is always a sprig of thyme, a few sprigs of parsley, and two bay leaves tied into a small bunch.

Mixed herbs are bought dried, ready mixed, and contain rubbed parsley, celery, savoury, marjoram, thyme, and sage.

Pepper is always freshly ground black pepper.

Butter is always salted, unless otherwise indicated.

We have been as careful as we can, and Mrs. Manders has toiled long hours, trying to make the recipes clear, but the reader must remember they are intended for those who know something of cooking and take real interest in it. I know the dishes only from eating them, and indeed they are "lovely."

PUBLISHERS' NOTE: *The recipes have been edited to convert Mrs. Manders' British measurements into American equivalents, and terms that may be unfamiliar to American readers are explained parenthetically or in footnotes.*

GENERAL RECIPES

PUFF PASTRY

> 1½ cups (¾ lb.) butter
> 3½ cups flour
> ½ teaspoon salt
> juice of 1 lemon
> 1 cup ice water

METHOD: Divide the butter into three equal parts and chill. Sift the flour and salt together into a mixing bowl. Add the lemon juice to the cold water and mix lightly into the flour to form a dough. Sprinkle a pastry board or marble slab with a little flour—just enough to prevent the paste from sticking. (Be careful not to use too much flour during the rolling-out process.) Roll the paste out into a rectangle about ½ inch thick. Cut one of the portions of butter into small pieces and dot them lightly and evenly over the paste. Sprinkle over them a little more flour and fold the shorter edges of the paste in to the centre. Refrigerate for 15 minutes. Roll pastry out again and repeat the process with the second portion of butter, omitting the flour. Fold as before and chill for another 15 minutes. Repeat the procedure with the third piece of butter. Roll the chilled pastry out for a fourth time; fold and chill again. Repeat the rolling, folding, and chilling procedure twice more, and leave the pastry in the refrigerator for a final half-hour before using. Makes approximately 2 pounds uncooked pastry.

SHORT PASTRY

> 2 cups self-raising flour
> ½ teaspoon salt
> ⅔ cup butter or margarine
> 1 egg
> juice of ½ lemon
> about 4 tablespoons ice water or cold milk

METHOD: Sift the flour and salt into a mixing bowl. Rub in the fat with your fingers until the mixture resembles crumbs. Beat the egg. Make a hole in the centre of the dry mixture, and add the beaten egg and lemon juice. Add just enough water or milk to make it possible to knead all together into a smooth dough. The dryer the dough the better. Makes about 1 pound uncooked pastry.

When making pastry that is to be served cold, I always use milk for moistening it. The pastry will keep short and crisp longer than if it is mixed with water.

BÉCHAMEL SAUCE

> 3 tablespoons butter
> 2½ tablespoons flour
> 2½ cups hot (not boiling) milk
> salt and pepper

METHOD: Melt the butter in a saucepan on fairly low heat. Stir in the flour and keep stirring until smooth, then add, little by little, the heated milk, stirring constantly until the mixture starts to bubble. Season to taste and cook over low heat for 5 to 10 minutes, stirring constantly. Makes about 2½ cups.

If the sauce is made in advance, cover with a lid to prevent a skin forming.

This is the basic sauce for cheese sauce, egg-and-parsley sauce, mushroom sauce, shrimp sauce, and so forth.

MY MAYONNAISE

2 egg yolks
¾ teaspoon dry mustard
¾ teaspoon salt
1¼ teaspoon sugar
1¼ cups olive oil
1¼ teaspoons tarragon vinegar
1¼ teaspoons white wine vinegar
2½ tablespoons cream

METHOD: Put the raw egg yolks into a bowl; be sure that all the white has been eliminated. Add the mustard, salt, and sugar, and mix thoroughly with a wooden spoon. Add the oil slowly, drop by drop, stirring well all the time, until the mixture becomes the consistency of thick cream. Still stirring constantly, add the oil a little faster, in a thin stream, until all is added. The mixture should be stiff. Add the vinegar and, last, the cream. Makes about 1¾ cups.

MY SALAD DRESSING

½ teaspoon mustard
2 teaspoons finely granulated sugar
1 teaspoon Worcestershire sauce
1 teaspoon wine vinegar
2 tablespoons olive oil
½ teaspoon salt
1 teaspoon lemon juice
1 teaspoon tarragon vinegar
1 tablespoon cream or top milk

METHOD: Put the ingredients, in the order given, into a screw-top jar. Put on the lid and shake vigorously until all is thoroughly blended and smooth. Makes about ¾ cup. Store in a cool place and use when required.

VINAIGRETTE DRESSING

½ teaspoon each finely chopped gherkin,
    shallot, parsley
½ teaspoon salt
½ teaspoon pepper
sugar to taste
4 tablespoons olive oil
1 tablespoon tarragon vinegar

METHOD: Mix all well together. Makes about ⅔ cup.

These recipes for mayonnaise and salad dressings always make me think of the days when I used to be called on to put up cold luncheons for shooting parties. In one of my posts we used to go to Yorkshire every season, as my employers had an estate there. It was a nice change to be away from London, but these parties entailed a lot of extra work.

Several days a week would find me and my assistants making all sorts of delectable dishes to be packed carefully into hampers by the butler. We prepared game pie, veal-and-ham pie, cold roasted chickens from the farm, cold guinea fowl, pâtés and terrines, salmon mousse, prawns with peas and sliced tomatoes in aspic, all kinds of sandwiches. Flasks of hot soup went too, and flasks of coffee, to say nothing of bottles of wine. We made miniature pats of butter that were put into a silver-topped container, to go with rolls of white bread. I always sent green salad, and the dressings were put into silver-topped bottles: I remember impressing on the butler that the dressing must be well shaken up before a bottle was opened.

No sweet was ever asked for, and very seldom was anything brought back uneaten to my kitchen. I remember thinking, "Where on earth do they put it all?"

TO CLARIFY DRIPPING

Chop the dripping and put it into a saucepan with enough water to cover it. Let it boil without a lid on until the liquid no longer looks silky but is oily. Cool a little, then strain through a coarse piece of cloth into a clean bowl.

CROÛTES AND CROÛTONS

For croûtes, cut slices of bread into rounds of the desired size. Fry gently in butter until browned on both sides. Drain well. Use white bread unless otherwise specified in recipe.

For croûtons, cut stale slices of bread into cubes and fry in plenty of butter until golden; then drain well, sprinkle with chopped parsley, and serve.

To freshen stale bread, sprinkle a little milk over the stale loaf and put into a warm, not hot, oven for a few minutes.

HORS D'OEUVRES

GRAPEFRUIT WITH RUM

½ grapefruit per person
finely granulated sugar
1 teaspoon rum per person
Maraschino cherries

METHOD: Cut grapefruit in halves, remove segments carefully, and keep the empty shells on one side. Put the segments and juice into a bowl with a little sugar, and cover with rum. Cover the bowl and leave the segments to soak for a few hours.

Remove all pith from the shells and place them in serving dishes. Put the segments, with the liquid in which they have been soaking, into a pan over gentle heat. Bring just to boiling point. Spoon the fruit into the shells and place a Maraschino cherry in the centre of each. Serve at once.

Most people expect grapefruit to be cold, so this recipe gives a pleasant surprise, especially in winter. At Warwick Castle when I served this, the butler used to come out and tell me it had made the men purr! I have an idea that most men don't care for chilled grapefruit.

FONDUE DE BÂLE

1 *lb. Gruyère cheese*
2 *teaspoons butter*
2 *cups dry white wine*
2 *tablespoons Kirsch*
1 *teaspoon dry French vermouth*

METHOD: Cut the cheese into small pieces and heat with the butter over hot water until they melt and blend; stir carefully and gradually add the white wine. Keep stirring and add the Kirsch; continue to stir and finally add the dry vermouth. Serves 6.

Fondue should not be served on plates; serve it in a communal bowl over a spirit lamp to keep fondue warm but not so hot as to scorch it. With it serve bread cut into cubes; each person spears a cube on his fork, dips it into the fondue, and eats.

A dry white wine—I prefer a Riesling—well chilled, should be drunk with this dish.

MACÉDOINE NIÇOISE

¼ lb. cold cooked chicken
4 thin slices lean boiled ham
2 thin slices mortadella sausage
4 oz. smoked herring in oil
whites of 2 hard-cooked eggs
1 large beet, cooked
3 medium potatoes, boiled, peeled, and cooled
½ apple
½ stalk celery
1 green pepper
6 pitted ripe olives
1 head lettuce
salt and pepper to taste

METHOD: Cut the chicken, ham, mortadella, and herring into long strips. Cut up finely the whites of egg, beet, potatoes, apple, celery, green pepper, olives, and lettuce. Mix all together. Season well and dress with Sauce Ravigote (see index). Serves 6.

SAUCE RAVIGOTE

2 teaspoons dry mustard
yolks of 2 hard-cooked eggs, pounded to a
    paste
salt and pepper
4 tablespoons olive oil
1 tablespoon chopped parsley and chervil
1 tablespoon wine vinegar

METHOD: Mix all together, whipping well. Makes about ⅔ cup.

TOMATO ICE CREAM

2 teaspoons butter
2 teaspoons flour
2 cups milk
4 tablespoons tomato purée
juice of ½ lemon

> salt and pepper to taste
> 1 tablespoon finely granulated sugar
> 4 tablespoons cream
> savoury biscuits, lettuce leaves, and watercress
>   to garnish
> 3 pitted ripe olives

METHOD: Melt the butter and stir in the flour over moderate heat. Add milk and tomato purée gradually, stirring, until the sauce is a deep salmon colour and tastes strongly of tomato—strongly, as it will lose a little flavour as it freezes. Cook the mixture until very smooth and until it "breathes" or bubbles, stirring constantly. Remove from heat, stir in the lemon juice, salt, pepper, and sugar. Beware of putting in too much sugar, as the mixture should have a definite sweet-sour flavour and be rather highly seasoned. Let it cool, then stir in the cream.

Put in the freezing compartment of the refrigerator for 1 hour or more, according to the coldness of the refrigerator. This ice cream gets very solid, so before serving take it out, put in a bowl, and mash well with a fork (this is important). Serve in glasses on a bed of shredded lettuce leaves; place half an olive on top and two biscuits on each side. The flavour improves if the filled glasses can be left in the refrigerator (but not in the freezing compartment) for about 20 minutes. Serves 6.

WATER-LILY EGGS

> 8 tablespoons butter
> 6 slices whole-wheat bread
> 6 eggs
> ½ cup grated Cheddar or Gruyère cheese
> salt and pepper

METHOD: Preheat oven to 300°. Melt 2 tablespoons butter in frying pan. Cut a circular piece from each slice of bread. Fry the circles nice and brown on both sides and keep hot on an ovenproof serving dish or on small individual dishes. Separate eggs, putting all whites together, but keeping each yolk separate. Beat the whites until very stiff, and pile on the rounds of bread. Make a hole in the centre of each mound, drop in ½ tablespoon butter, and carefully drop in an egg yolk. Sprinkle with grated cheese and salt and pepper, and add another ½ tablespoon butter. Bake for 1 hour. Increase heat for a few minutes to brown the egg whites. Serve at once. Serves 6.

CHEESE BOUCHÉES

> ½ lb. puff pastry (see index)
> 1¼ tablespoons flour
> 2½ cups milk
> 3 eggs, beaten
> 1½ cups grated cheese
> salt and pepper

METHOD: Preheat oven to 400°. Grease a baking sheet. Roll out puff pastry until it is about ½ inch thick. With a 2-inch pastry cutter, make six rounds. With a 1½-inch cutter, make a slight indentation in each round and place the rounds on the baking sheet, about 2 inches apart. Bake for about ½ hour, or until doubled in size and golden brown. Remove top from each puff and cut out damp centre carefully with a spoon. Cool. Reset oven at 450°.

Mix the flour with a little of the milk. Add the beaten eggs, the rest of the milk, cheese, and seasoning. Heat the mixture gently in a double boiler until it thickens, stirring constantly. Fill pastry cases with mixture and put into oven for 15 to 20 minutes. Serve hot. Serves 6.

CHEESE STRAWS

> 1¼ cups self-raising flour
> pinch of salt
> ⅛ teaspoon paprika
> ¾ cup butter
> 1 cup grated Parmesan cheese
> juice of ½ lemon
> ice water
> 1 egg, beaten
> paprika for dusting

METHOD: Preheat oven to 400°. Grease a baking sheet. Sift the flour with the salt and paprika. Rub in the butter with your fingertips until the mixture resembles coarse crumbs. Add the grated cheese. Add lemon juice and just enough ice water to make a soft dough. Roll pastry out thin. Cut a few rings about 4 inches in diameter; cut the rest into 4-inch strips and twist them. Lay the straws and rings on baking sheet. Brush with beaten egg, dust with paprika, and bake until golden, 10 to 15 minutes. Cool on racks. Arrange the straws in small bundles inside the rings. Serves 12.

Just as my salad dressings make me remember those shooting-party days on the Yorkshire moors, making cheese straws brings back our going up there for the fox-hunting season.

My employer was Master of a well-known pack, and at least twice in a season the meet was outside our big house. The riders would assemble to wait until the hounds arrived, and the hospitality offered was lavish. The butler and I would go out carrying trays and salvers. I had cheese straws, canapés, slabs of hot gingerbread, sausages on toothpicks— made locally, they were sausages to remember! The butler had glasses of sloe gin and steaming toddy.

It was a grand sight: the pink coats of the men; the beautifully fitting habits of the ladies, so well groomed, their hair netted under their top hats or bowlers; the hounds' tails waving; the horses arching their necks and pawing the gravel, a lovely gloss on their coats; the children bundled up on their Shetland ponies. I was nervous, though, of going among the horses, especially the kickers, which had red ribbons on their tails.

CHEESE SOUFFLÉ

2 tablespoons butter
2 tablespoons flour
1½ cups hot milk
1 cup grated cheese
4 eggs, separated
salt and pepper to taste

METHOD: Preheat oven to 400°. Melt the butter in a pan, add the flour, stirring well with a wooden spoon, over moderate heat, and add the hot milk gradually. Cook, stirring, until thickened. Stir in grated cheese until melted. Remove from heat, cool slightly, and add egg yolks. Season with a little salt and black pepper. Allow to cool. Then beat the egg whites until they are stiff and fold them in carefully. Butter a 1½-quart soufflé dish, pour in the mixture, and place in the oven. Immediately lower heat to 375°. Bake for 25 to 30 minutes, or until soufflé is well risen and browned. Serves 4.

Instead of cheese, cooked spinach (fresh or frozen), crab, or flaked sole may be used.

GNOCCHI ALLA ROMANA

> 2 lbs. potatoes, peeled
> salt
> ½ cup butter
> 1¾ cups flour
> 2 eggs, well beaten
> salt and pepper
> grated Parmesan cheese
> 3 tablespoons melted butter

METHOD: Preheat oven to 300°. Grease 2 fireproof dishes and warm them. Boil potatoes in salted water for 20 minutes. Drain and mash with ¼ cup butter. Gradually incorporate the flour, beaten eggs, and seasoning. Roll between floured hands into rolls the thickness of a finger and cut into pieces 1 inch long. Bring a pan of salted water to a boil, drop the gnocchi gently into the pan, one by one, and boil for 3 or 4 minutes, until they rise to the top. The water should boil gently, not furiously.

Remove the gnocchi with a perforated spoon to a hot greased fireproof dish. Dot with 1 tablespoon of remaining butter and keep warm in the oven long enough to allow the butter to melt and give the gnocchi an attractive glazed appearance. Into another hot fireproof dish put a layer of gnocchi, liberally sprinkle with grated Parmesan cheese, and dot with butter.

Add a second and third layer in the same way, piling the layers in pyramid form. After sprinkling the last layer with Parmesan cheese, pour melted butter over all. Place in oven for 20 minutes, or until pale golden in colour. Serve hot. Serves 8.

SMOKED SALMON SWEDISH STYLE

½ lb. smoked salmon, sliced
4 eggs
2 tablespoons butter
2½ tablespoons milk
salt and pepper
1 teaspoon chopped parsley
5 teaspoons chopped pimiento
1 teaspoon chopped capers

METHOD: Cut salmon into pieces 2 inches wide, 4 inches long. Roll each piece up and arrange round the edge of a serving platter. Break eggs into a saucepan, add butter and milk, and season to taste. Stir over low heat until the eggs begin to scramble. Remove from heat while they are still soft. Quickly add the parsley and pimiento, stir, and pile eggs up in the centre of the salmon. Sprinkle with chopped capers, chill, and serve very cold. Serves 4.

HAM CORNETS

1 cup cold vegetables cut into neat dice
  (carrots, potatoes, peas, and beans)
2 tablespoons mayonnaise (see index)
6 thin slices cooked ham
lettuce leaves to garnish

METHOD: Mix the diced vegetables with the mayonnaise. Roll each piece of ham into the shape of a cornet and fill with the vegetable mixture. If necessary, secure the cornets with toothpicks. Arrange on a round plate, with the points of the cornets pointing towards the centre. Garnish with lettuce leaves. Makes 6 cornets.

PRAWN COCKTAILS

crisp inside lettuce leaves
½ lb. tiny shrimp, cooked
64 prawns (large shrimp), cooked
½ teaspoon dry mustard
1 teaspoon finely granulated sugar
pinch of salt
squeeze of lemon juice
1 tablespoon wine vinegar
2 tablespoons olive oil
1 tablespoon cream
1 teaspoon Worcestershire sauce
1 teaspoon tomato ketchup
few dashes of Tabasco sauce

METHOD: Arrange cleaned crisp inside leaves of lettuce in eight sundae glasses so as to make an attractive surround, and in the centre of each put a pile of small shrimp. On top, in the centre, put a tiny lettuce leaf. Arrange over the side of each glass, between the leaves, eight large prawns, with the heads facing inwards. Just before serving, mix together the mustard, sugar, salt, lemon juice, and vinegar. Add the oil, cream, Worcestershire sauce, ketchup, and three or four shakes of Tabasco sauce. Mix and beat all together vigorously. Spoon over the cocktails and serve. Serves 8.

This sauce can conveniently be made in a screw-top jar, and, once made, keeps indefinitely in the refrigerator.

LOBSTER COCKTAIL

1 cup cooked lobster meat
½ teaspoon chopped chives
2 teaspoons Worcestershire sauce
¼ cup tomato ketchup
¼ cup lemon juice
½ teaspoon Tabasco sauce
salt and pepper to taste
lettuce leaves, lemon slices, and small shrimp
   to garnish

METHOD: Flake lobster meat into a bowl and add the other ingredients, except for the garnish. Mix lightly together and serve in sundae glasses that have been prepared as for prawn cocktail (see index). Decorate with small lettuce leaves, lemon slices, and small shrimp. Serves 4.

CAVIAR WITH SHRIMP

> 6 thin slices brown bread, buttered
> 1 lemon, sliced
> 1½ ozs. black caviar
> ½ shallot
> a few drops lemon juice
> Cayenne pepper
> 2 tablespoons capers
> 24 small cooked shrimp, fresh or frozen

METHOD: Remove the crusts from the bread, cut out six rounds of about 1½ inches in diameter, and cover each with a thin slice of lemon trimmed to the size of the round. Put caviar in a small bowl. Chop the shallot finely and add with lemon juice. Season with Cayenne and stir with a wooden spoon. Pile this mixture on the rounds, then, with the point of a wooden skewer or toothpick, hollow the centre down to the lemon and fill the cavity with capers. Arrange four shrimp in an upright position on each round and serve. Serves 6.

This, of course, is a dish for really grand occasions.

SOUPS

Stock, as Miss Godden says in her preface, can be made from anything (and *should* be made, to avoid waste): chicken carcasses, vegetable water (but not water from cabbage, broccoli, or Brussels sprouts), leftover gravy, the stock from boiled meat (especially ham, and I always keep a bit of the rind as well, for this gives an excellent taste to lentils or beans). I also keep soured cream for soups (and for sauces as well), and bacon rind, which adds flavour.

Stock with different flavours, i.e., chicken, beef, ham, should be kept in separate bowls or jugs.

LENTIL SOUP

2 cups lentils
1 large onion
3 tablespoons butter
4 cups stock (preferably chicken or ham)
salt and pepper

METHOD: Soak the lentils overnight in water to cover. Peel and slice the onion finely, melt 1½ tablespoons butter in a large heavy pan, add onion, and sauté gently until golden. Remove from heat, add stock and lentils, and season to taste. Return to heat, bring to the boil, and simmer very, very gently, partially covered. Stir quite frequently until the lentils have become a smooth mass (about 1 hour). Before serving, beat in 1½ tablespoons butter. Serves 4 to 6.

Any scraps of bacon or ham and, if possible, a ham bone can be added to this soup during the cooking process and removed before serving.

In one of my posts I became friendly with a Scotswoman who was a marvellous cook. She was a fat motherly soul and the essence of cleanliness. I used to go and see her sometimes in the evenings, and she would produce this lentil soup, accompanied by her own new-made bread. This sounds a simple meal, but, as made by her, it was ambrosia! Good cooks are often chary of giving recipes away, but this kindly woman showed me how to make the soup. The recipe seems as simple as the soup, but the first time I made it I had a failure: I had boiled, not simmered, it. Now I place an asbestos mat under the pan so that the simmer is exceedingly gentle—which is why I stress that in the recipe —and the soup is quite perfect.

POTAGE VÉRONIQUE

 4 small tomatoes
 2 tablespoons rice
 4 tablespoons butter
 2 onions, peeled
 5 teaspoons tomato purée
 1 bay leaf
 1 clove garlic, crushed
 a few peppercorns
 salt
 4 cups stock or bouillon made from cubes
 1 tablespoon chopped parsley
 1 teaspoon sugar

METHOD: Cut up 3 tomatoes coarsely, leaving skins on. Cook the rice 10 minutes in boiling salted water. Melt the butter in a stew pan, slice in the onions, and add the cut-up tomatoes, tomato purée, bay leaf, garlic, peppercorns, and a little salt. Cover the pan and cook slowly for 10 minutes, stirring occasionally. Remove from heat, rub the mixture through a sieve into a fresh pan, and add the stock. Stir over heat until the whole comes to the boil. Now add rice and simmer again for 15 minutes. Skin the remaining tomato, remove seeds, and cut into shreds. In the last few minutes, add to the soup with the chopped parsley and sugar. Serves 4 to 6.

Serve the soup with Mornay toast (see index).

MORNAY TOAST

 bread, sliced wafer thin
 grated Parmesan cheese
 paprika

METHOD: Preheat oven to 350°. Cut the crusts from the bread slices, lay the slices on a baking sheet, sprinkle well with cheese, and dust with paprika. Put in oven till brown, about 10 minutes.

LA SOUPE À L'OIGNON GRATINÉE

6 large onions
3 tablespoons cooking oil
4 teaspoons flour
pepper and coarse salt to taste
4 slices French bread
4 tablespoons grated Gruyère cheese
4 eggs (optional)

METHOD: Peel and chop onions as finely as possible and sauté slowly in oil over low heat—use an asbestos pad if necessary—until soft and golden. Done properly, this should take about ½ hour, and burning or blackening the onions means failure. Then sprinkle in the flour and stir until flour turns pale brown. Turn up the heat so that the mixture boils, then immediately reduce heat. Add salt and pepper. Pour in 2¼ cups water gradually, stirring all the time. Bring to a simmer, reduce heat, and keep soup hot.

Put the French bread under the broiler briefly to dry it. Spread it thickly with grated Gruyère cheese, put soup into heatproof bowls, float one slice of bread on top of each, and put under broiler, about 2 inches from the flame, until cheese is golden-brown and bubbling.

Or, if this soup is to be presented "Belgian-fashion," put the boiling hot soup into bowls and break 1 egg into each. The eggs will immediately start to poach. Put cheese-spread bread slices on top of them and broil until brown. The egg comes as a pleasant surprise. Serves 4.

SOUP MAIGRE

2 onions
1 tablespoon parsley
1 tablespoon butter
2 water biscuits, crushed
1 small cabbage or 1 head lettuce, finely sliced
5 cups milk
1 egg, beaten
salt and pepper

METHOD: Chop onions and parsley finely and cook in butter over low heat for 15 minutes, shaking the pan frequently. Stir in the crushed biscuits and the finely sliced cabbage or lettuce and continue to cook and shake for another 10 minutes. Heat the milk just to the boiling point and add. Let simmer for ¾ hour over low heat, partially covered. Finally remove from heat, stir in the beaten egg, and season to taste. Serves 8.

BORSCH

6 large leeks
2 heads endive
4 large onions
4 medium beets, cooked
3 tablespoons butter
1¼ cups liquid from cooking beets
up to 5 tablespoons chopped beef, bacon,
    duck, or sausage scraps
salt and pepper
5 tablespoons heavy cream or sour cream

METHOD: Clean leeks and endive, peel onion, and cut these and the cooked beets into thin strips. Sauté vegetables in butter in a heavy-bottomed pan. Add 1¼ cups water and all but 2 tablespoons of the beet water. Bring to a boil and simmer until the leeks and endive are cooked (about ½ hour). Then add cold pieces of beef, duck, bacon, or sausage. Skim if necessary and colour at the last moment with 2 tablespoons beet water. Season and serve hot with blobs of cream, sour if preferred. Serves 8.

JERUSALEM ARTICHOKE SOUP

1 lb. Jerusalem artichokes
1 teaspoon vinegar
2 tablespoons butter
3¾ cups beef stock or bouillon
⅔ cup milk, heated
salt and pepper

METHOD: Scrub, peel, and halve the Jerusalem artichokes. Put in water to which vinegar has been added to keep them white. Leave for 10 minutes or so. Melt the butter in a saucepan and toss the artichokes in it for a few minutes. Then add the stock, bring to a boil, and simmer, partially covered, for 20 minutes or until the artichokes are tender. Rub soup through a hair sieve, or blend in a blender, add the heated milk, reheat (without boiling), and season to taste. Serves 6.

POTATO SOUP WITH CELERIAC

2 lbs. medium-sized potatoes
1 small celeriac (celery root)
2½ cups beef stock or bouillon
1 tablespoon butter
salt and pepper
½ to 1 cup milk

METHOD: Peel and slice the potatoes and celeriac and simmer in the stock until tender, about 20 minutes. Add the butter and season. Rub through a sieve or blend in blender. Thin with milk if too thick, heat but do not boil, and serve with croûtons (see index). Serves 6.

MARROW-BALLS SOUP

2 thick slices bread
¾ cup beef marrow
1 egg
pinch of nutmeg
salt and pepper
2 teaspoons flour
4 cups beef stock

METHOD: Remove crusts from the bread, soak the slices in water, and squeeze out moisture. Cream the marrow with a fork in a pan over hot water and mix with the soaked bread, egg, seasoning, and flour. Let the mixture cool, then form into balls about ¾ inch across. About 10 minutes before serving, heat the stock to boiling point and drop in the marrow balls, taking great care not to break them. Simmer gently for 10 minutes and serve. Serves 6.

BOUILLABAISSE

3 onions, finely chopped
4 cloves garlic, crushed
3 tomatoes, peeled, halved, and seeded
bouquet garni of parsley, thyme, bay leaf,
    fennel
1 piece orange peel
1 lb. firm-fleshed fish, cut in chunks *
½ cup olive oil
salt and pepper
¾ teaspoon nutmeg
¾ teaspoon saffron
1 lb. soft-fleshed fish, cut in chunks **
6 slices bread
extra olive oil
1 clove garlic, cut
2 tablespoons chopped parsley

METHOD: Put in a large saucepan the onions, garlic, tomatoes, bouquet garni, and orange peel. On this bed put pieces of fish with firm flesh. Pour the oil over them, add hot water to cover, season with salt, pepper, nutmeg, and saffron. Bring to the boil and cook, uncovered, over very high heat for 5 minutes. Now put in softer-fleshed fish and cook 5 minutes more. Remove bouquet garni. Drain fish, reserving liquid. Sauté bread in olive oil and rub with garlic. Pour fish liquid over bread and serve as soup. Serve the pieces of fish, sprinkled all over with chopped parsley, in another dish. Serves 6.

SPINACH SOUP

1 lb. spinach
salt
2½ tablespoons oil
1 clove garlic, crushed
2½ tablespoons flour
5 cups stock
croûtons (see index)
grated Parmesan cheese

* Such as halibut, eel, crab, or lobster.
** Such as whiting, mullet, flounder, smelts.

METHOD: Wash the spinach, cook it in a very small quantity of boiling salted water, and purée in a blender or put through a food mill. Heat oil in a pan and add the garlic; when it is brown, remove. Mix in the flour. Add the spinach purée and the stock. Bring to the boil and simmer for ½ hour, partially covered. Serve with croûtons and cheese. Serves 6.

MUSHROOM SOUP

1 onion
1 lb. mushrooms, sliced
2 tablespoons butter
5 cups chicken stock, heated
1¼ tablespoons potato flour
2½ tablespoons cream
⅔ cup whipped cream

METHOD: Peel and chop the onion and cook with the mushrooms in the butter until tender, about 15 minutes. Add the chicken stock. Simmer for 10 minutes, then pass through a sieve or blend in blender. Just before serving, mix potato flour with cream and stir into soup. Reheat over low heat. Serve with blobs of whipped cream. Serves 6 to 8.

MIMOSA SOUP

boiling water
¼ cup rice
2½ cups stock or bouillon
2½ cups milk
1¼ teaspoons sugar
salt to taste
yolks of 4 hard-cooked eggs

METHOD: Pour boiling water over rice, then rinse in plenty of cold water and drain. Cook the rice very slowly in the stock and milk for 1 hour, partially covered, then add the sugar and salt. Just before serving, rub the egg yolks through a sieve and sprinkle on top. Serves 6.

This is one of the prettiest soups I have ever seen—if "pretty" is a word one can use to describe soup. To my mind it has an especial appeal if served in spring, when one can put spring flowers on the table: daffodils, jonquils, narcissi. The eye is very much charmed.

GOLDEN SOUP

> 2 young vegetable marrows (summer squash),
>   about 8 inches long
> 5 cups stock
> ⅔ cup cream, heated
> salt and pepper
> croûtons (see index)

METHOD: Peel and slice the squash; simmer them in the stock until tender, 10 to 15 minutes. Rub them through a sieve, or blend in blender. Reheat, and just before serving stir in the heated cream and seasoning. Serve with croûtons. Serves 6 to 8.

RICE AND SORREL SOUP

> ½ cup rice
> ¼ cup powdered sorrel or 1 cup shredded fresh
>   sorrel
> 5 cups stock
> 1¼ cups milk or cream
> pinch of nutmeg
> salt and pepper
> 1 egg, beaten (optional)

METHOD: Cook rice and sorrel in the stock until tender, about 20 minutes. Add the milk or cream and nutmeg. Season and mix well. The soup is improved by the addition of a well-beaten egg before serving, but if this is used it must not boil again. Serves 6 to 8.

FISH

SAUMON BRETON

> 2 lbs. fresh salmon
> salt and pepper
> 4 tablespoons butter
> ½ lb. mushrooms, sliced
> parsley, chopped
> juice of ½ lemon

METHOD: Preheat oven to 375°. The only difficult part of this dish is removing the bones and skin from the salmon, but most fishmongers will do this if asked. If it is done at home, however, be sure to use a very sharp knife; otherwise the fish will flake. Proceed carefully, and allow plenty of time.

When skin and bones are removed, the fish should be in two fillets. Cut it into 2-inch cubes; again, use a very sharp knife. Sprinkle with salt and pepper. Melt 3 tablespoons butter in a pan and toss the salmon pieces in it together with the mushrooms until the fish is half cooked—about 7 minutes. Then move the pan to the oven to finish cooking—about 10 minutes more. Drain well, put fish and mushrooms in a serving dish, sprinkle with chopped parsley, and keep warm. Putting 1 tablespoon butter into a hot pan over low heat, add any butter left over from cooking the fish. In a minute or so the butter will take colour and become a light golden brown. Add a little lemon juice and pour over the fish. This is *beurre meunière*. (It is essential not to let it get to the black stage and become *beurre noir*, which is used for other kinds of dishes.) Serves 4 to 5.

GALANTINE DE SAUMON

2 lbs. salmon
salt and pepper
about 1¼ cups sherry
1 lb. white fish, preferably fresh haddock
1 slice stale bread dipped in milk
yolks of 2 eggs
2 tablespoons butter, melted

METHOD: Cut the salmon into slices 1 inch thick; put them into a dish and marinate for 2 hours with salt, pepper, and enough sherry to cover them.

Preheat oven to 350°. To make the stuffing, mince together the white fish and the stale bread; add salt and pepper, egg yolks, butter, and ¼ cup of the sherry in which the salmon has been marinating. Butter a shallow casserole and place in it the slices of salmon and the stuffing in alternate layers. Cover and bake in the oven for 1¼ hours. Serve hot or cold. Serves 8.

SOLE MAYONNAISE

> 1¼ cups milk
> 1 teaspoon salt
> 6 large fillets of sole
> 6 eggs
> extra milk
> salt and pepper
> lemon juice to taste
> 1¼ cup mayonnaise (see index)

METHOD: Mix together milk, 1¼ cups water, and salt. Place the fillets in a fireproof dish, cover with the liquid, and slowly bring to the boil; simmer gently until done, about 10 minutes. Drain fillets and cool. Hard-cook the eggs, shell, and mash the yolks with a little milk; add pepper, salt, and lemon juice to taste. Heap the mixture in the centre of a serving dish and arrange fillets round it. Spread a thin layer of mayonnaise over the whole and decorate with chopped egg white. Chill and serve very cold. Serves 6.

FILETS DE SOLE MÂCONNAISE

> 6 large fillets of sole (ask the fishmonger for
>   the heads and bones)
> 2 onions, sliced
> salt and pepper
> bouquet garni (see index)
> ⅔ cup red Burgundy
> ¼ lb. button mushrooms
> 3 tablespoons milk
> 2 teaspoons flour
> 2 tablespoons butter

METHOD: Place fish heads and bones in a flat pan with onions, a little salt and pepper, the bouquet garni, wine, and ⅓ cup water. Bring to the boil and simmer for 10 minutes over low heat. Put in the fillets to poach. Simmer until done—about 15 minutes—drain, and keep hot. Let the sauce reduce over low heat for a few minutes longer. Meanwhile, cook the button mushrooms in milk and 3 tablespoons water until tender. Drain and keep hot.

Pass the sauce from the fish through a fine strainer into a small pan. Work the flour into a paste with 1 tablespoon butter and add to the sauce. Stir over low heat until smooth. Now add, just at the end, 1 tablespoon butter, season to taste, and stir. The sauce should have the consistency of cream. Arrange the fillets in a long serving dish with the mushrooms around them. Pour the sauce over them. Serves 6.

BAKED FILLETS WITH TOMATOES

8 medium tomatoes
1 medium onion
8 fillets of sole or plaise (flounder)
salt and pepper
1½ tablespoons milk
⅓ cup dry white wine
1½ tablespoons grated Parmesan cheese

METHOD: Preheat oven to 350°. Butter a fireproof dish. Skin and slice the tomatoes, chop the onion, and mix together. Season the fillets; spread the onion and tomatoes over them. Fold the fillets over and place them in the buttered dish with the milk and wine. Sprinkle the grated cheese over, cover with buttered paper or foil, and bake for 20 minutes. Remove the buttered paper or foil for the last 5 minutes to allow the sauce to brown nicely. Serves 4.

HALIBUT STEAKS

1½ lbs. halibut
juice of ½ lemon
salt and pepper

METHOD: Preheat oven to 350°. Wash fish and cut it into ½-inch-thick slices. Butter a baking tin, lay fish slices on this. Pour the lemon juice over them and sprinkle with salt and pepper. Cover with buttered paper or foil and bake 15 minutes. Remove and place in a hot serving dish and cover with Maître d'Hôtel Sauce (see index). Serves 6.

MAÎTRE D'HÔTEL SAUCE

> 1 tablespoon butter
> ½ teaspoon chopped shallot
> 1 tablespoon flour
> 1¼ cups stock
> 1¼ cups milk
> salt and pepper
> 2 teaspoons chopped parsley
> 1¼ teaspoon lemon juice

METHOD: Melt butter in a pan, add the shallot, and cook gently for 10 minutes. Stir in the flour gradually, then add the stock and milk slowly, stirring all the time. Add salt and pepper to taste, then the chopped parsley, and lastly the lemon juice. (Any gravy that has run from fish in cooking can also be added.) Makes about 2½ cups.

WHITING WITH PEAS

> 1 lb. peas, shelled
> salt
> 1 onion
> 1 tablespoon cooking oil
> 1 tablespoon chopped parsley
> 4 whiting, heads removed
> 1 tablespoon tomato purée, diluted with a few
>   drops boiling water

METHOD: Half-cook the peas in boiling salted water (about 3 minutes) and drain. Chop the onion finely. Heat the oil in a shallow pan and brown the onion, parsley, and whiting. When the fish is browned on both sides, add the peas and the tomato purée. Allow to cook, covered, for another 15 minutes over moderate heat, then serve. Serves 4.

In one of my posts there were three children in the nursery, and, knowing what a nutritious fish a whiting is, I thought the children ought to have it; but as most children cannot deal with fish bones or spines, I gave myself plenty of work for these three by filleting each whiting by hand and cooking the fillets in milk and butter. I was well rewarded, because the children liked whiting so much they asked for it at least once a week. What work it was!

CREAMED FRESH HADDOCK WITH ALMONDS

1½ lbs. fresh haddock
salt and pepper
3 tablespoons butter
2 tablespoons flour
1¼ tablespoons grated cheese
2½ cups stock in which fish has been cooked
2½ teaspoons cream
1¼ tablespoons dry white wine
1 tablespoon chopped parsley
2 tablespoons almonds, blanched and chopped roughly

METHOD: Preheat oven to 375°. Poach haddock, partially covered, in boiling salted water for 15 minutes. Remove fish and keep warm; keep stock for sauce. Melt butter, add flour and cheese, stir well. Add fish stock gradually, stirring until sauce thickens and bubbles. It is then cooked; season and remove from heat. Add the cream, wine, and parsley. Remove skin and bones from the cooked fish and put it into a mixing bowl; try not to break the fish up too much. Pour the sauce over it, mix carefully, and put into a fireproof dish. Sprinkle with the chopped almonds and bake for 10 minutes. If the almonds have not browned, finish off with a few minutes under a hot broiler. Serves 6.

FILLETS OF FISH MAÎTRE D'HÔTEL

6 to 8 fillets of sole or plaice (flounder)
2 teaspoons lemon juice
pepper to taste
1¼ cups béchamel sauce (see index)
1 tablespoon chopped parsley
lemon slices

METHOD: Bake fillets in a greased ovenproof dish at 350° for 15 minutes. When done, sprinkle with lemon juice and pepper. Place fillets on a hot serving dish and cover with béchamel sauce. Garnish with chopped parsley and lemon slices. Serves 4.

ARINGA ALLA GRATELLA

> 8 *medium-sized herrings*
> 1¼ *cups milk*
> 1 *tablespoon olive oil*
> *lemon slices*

METHOD: Clean the herrings, split them open, and remove the backbones. Lay on a flat dish and cover with cold milk; leave to soak for a couple of hours or overnight.

Drain, oil them lightly, and put under a hot broiler for 15 minutes. Serve with lemon slices. Serves 8.

RAIE À L'ORANGE

> 1½ *lbs. skate*
> ⅔ *cup red wine*
> 2 *teaspoons lemon juice*
> 2 *tablespoons melted butter*
> *bouquet garni (see index)*
> *salt and pepper*
> 3 *navel oranges*
> 5 *tablespoons butter*
> 2 *shallots, finely chopped*
> 1 *clove garlic, minced*
> 2 *teaspoons flour*
> 1 *tomato, cut up*
> ¼ *cup mushroom peelings and stalks*
> 1 *teaspoon tomato purée*
> 1 *tablespoon sherry*

METHOD: Preheat oven to 350°. Cut skate in strips, remove any dark skin, and place fish in a well-buttered ovenproof dish. Pour over it the red wine, 1½ cups water, lemon juice, and 2 tablespoons melted butter. Add bouquet garni and salt and pepper, cover with buttered paper or foil, and bake 20 minutes. Remove from oven, drain, reserving stock, and keep hot.

Shred the rind of one orange finely. Peel the other two oranges and cut into sections. Now melt 3 tablespoons butter in a pan; add salt and pepper, shallots, and garlic; sauté slowly until shallots are soft (about 10 minutes). Stir in flour and let brown slightly. Add the tomato, the mushroom peelings and stalks, and tomato purée; pour the fish stock over these and stir until boiling. Simmer for another 15 minutes, covered, and strain into another pan. Add sherry and orange rind, simmer another 5 minutes, and whisk in, bit by bit, 2 tablespoons butter. Keep hot.

Heat orange sections in a little butter. Arrange fish on serving dish, pour sauce over it, and surround with the orange sections. Serves 6.

Skate is not sufficiently appreciated in England; in fact most people think of it as suitable only for fish-and-chips shops and vans, whereas it can make most delicious and delicate dishes. This Raie à l'Orange is fit for the most recherché dinner; it is simple to make, but the result is delectable.

HOMARD À LA PLACE
ST. JAMES

> 1 2-lb. lobster, cooked
> 4 tablespoons butter
> 1 shallot
> ⅓ cup dry white wine
> salt and cayenne pepper to taste
> ½ teaspoon chopped parsley
> ⅔ cup Espagnole sauce (see index)
> 2½ teaspoons lemon juice

METHOD: Take the meat out of the lobster shell and cut into small pieces. Melt the butter, chop the shallot, and sauté till soft but not browned. Add the wine and allow to reduce a little over low heat. Stir in the lobster meat, seasoning, and chopped parsley. Cook over low heat for 5 minutes, stirring constantly. Place on a hot dish, cover with Espagnole sauce, and squeeze lemon juice over all. Serves 4.

ESPAGNOLE SAUCE FOR HOMARD À LA PLACE ST. JAMES

> 2 tablespoons butter
> 2 tablespoons raw lean ham or bacon, diced
> ½ onion
> ½ medium carrot
> 1 large mushroom
> bouquet garni (see index)
> 2 peppercorns
> 1 clove
> 2 tablespoons flour
> 2½ cups beef stock
> ⅓ cup tomato purée
> ⅓ cup sherry
> salt and pepper

METHOD: Melt the butter in a large heavy-bottomed pan, add the ham or bacon, and sauté for a few minutes. Finely slice the onion, carrot, and mushroom and add to the pan with the bouquet garni, peppercorns, and clove. Stir all together over low heat for 5 minutes; then add the flour gradually and stir till it has browned. Add the stock, tomato purée, and sherry, and bring to boiling point, stirring constantly. Then simmer, partially covered, for 1 hour. Skim off fat, season to taste, and strain. Reheat and use. Makes about 2½ cups. This sauce can be stored in the refrigerator in a jar and used as required.

This lobster dish has its name because it was served in a well-known club for gentlemen in Pall Mall (I have promised never to divulge which club it was). The recipe was given to me as a great favour by one of the chefs whom I met with Marcel.

For a short time I had a post with the family of an eminent surgeon whose wife prided herself very much on her discernment about food. One day she told me that her darling son, "an officer in the Guards," would be home for the weekend; he was fond of lobster, and she asked me if I knew of any way of serving this beyond the "eternal cold with mayonnaise." I replied that I had my own special way of cooking and serving lobster.

"Hot?" she asked.

"Hot, with a sauce."

Looking at me most dubiously, she said in her haughty way that she was sure no female cook could make a hot lobster dish that would compare with, for instance, the chef's at Prunier's. I was a little nettled but said nothing. That night I served my Homard à la Place St. James, and next morning she was all compliments and smiles, and inevitably: "Who taught you that?"

Compliments, smiles or not, I didn't like the lady and soon left.

[There is only one way to describe this dish: it is "golluptious."—R.G.]

SCAMPI LOMBARD

½ small onion
1 clove garlic
1 bay leaf
4 cloves
1 tablespoon chopped parsley
¾ teaspoon chopped fennel
⅓ cup wine vinegar
salt and pepper
40 shrimp, shelled

METHOD: Chop the onion, crush the garlic, and mix together with all the other ingredients except the shrimp in a large pan. Cook for 5 minutes over moderate heat. Add the shrimp, cover, and cook over medium heat for 15 minutes, stirring from time to time. Serve hot. Serves 4.

PILAU DE MOULES

> 6 tablespoons butter
> 2 small onions, sliced
> salt and pepper
> 1½ cups Patna rice *
> 3 cups fish stock
> 2 tablespoons grated Swiss cheese
> 1 qt. mussels
> ⅔ cup dry white wine
> 1 teaspoon lemon juice
> bouquet garni (see index)
> 2 tablespoons flour
> ⅔ cup milk
> 2½ tablespoons cream
> chopped parsley to garnish

METHOD: Preheat oven to 350°. Heat 2 tablespoons butter in a large heavy-bottomed pan, add onions, season, and sauté a few minutes. Add the rice and sauté a moment longer. Pour on stock, bring to boil, cover pan with greased paper, add the lid, and place on bottom shelf in oven for 20 minutes. Remove and with a fork stir in 2 tablespoons butter and the grated cheese. Keep warm.

Wash the mussels well and put into a large pan with the wine, 1¼ cups water, a little salt, lemon juice, and bouquet garni. Bring slowly to the boil and boil until the mussels open, tossing occasionally. Shell mussels, beard them, and put them in a pan to keep warm; leave the beards in the liquor and reserve, also keeping warm.

Melt 2 tablespoons butter, remove from heat, stir in flour, and season. Strain the mussel liquor and add it. Add the milk and stir over heat until boiling. Remove from heat and stir in cream. Moisten the mussels with a little of the sauce. Oil a 2-quart charlotte mould well and line with rice; fill the centre with the mussels and cover level with the remaining rice, pressing all well down. Let it rest for 3 or 4 minutes, then turn it out quickly onto a hot dish. Pour the rest of the sauce around and decorate the top with one or two mussels and chopped parsley. Serves 6 to 8.

* Carolina long-grain rice may be used.

The preceding dish is one Raymond taught me—I think I can safely say there is much of Raymond's influence in my cooking—but it took me quite a time to learn how to present a Pilau de Moules in the way he said was correct, so one mustn't be discouraged if for the first time or two it seems difficult. The recipe originally came from Scotland, where the mussels were cooked straight from the sea, which always gives them a special taste. Now we drive to Hastings, where I know some fishermen so get the mussels very fresh; but I have often had to make the pilau with mussels from the fishmonger; it is still good.

I remember when I was with the novelist Sheila Kaye-Smith we discussed a certain dinner-party menu and I suggested a Pilau de Moules. Her husband, Penrose—later Sir Penrose Fry—was avid to taste it, but unfortunately on the evening of the party he had to go to bed with a bad back. I was determined, however, that he should taste his Pilau de Moules and got ready a tray daintily laid with a nice portion of my pilau and a roll and pat of butter and a glass of red wine (red is best with mussels). Just as I was taking it up, one of the gentlemen guests appeared. "Is that for Penrose? I'll take it up."

I said, "The stairs are awkward and uncarpeted, and highly polished. Best let me."

He insisted, though courteously, but a moment later there was a crash—mussels, wine, china, glass, all in a smash, butter smeared everywhere, and the roll bouncing down the stairs. Luckily I had made enough pilau for the whole party and several more, and in the end Mr. Fry did get his dish.

FISH SCALLOPS

2 cups any cold cooked flaked fish, without bones
1 cup cold cooked chopped vegetables (peas, beans, carrots, potatoes)
salt and pepper
paprika
⅔ cup mayonnaise (see index)

METHOD: Arrange flaked fish and chopped vegetables in scallop shells. Season to taste, sprinkle a little paprika over them, and cover generously with a layer of mayonnaise. Serve cold. Serves 4.

MEAT

ESCALOPES DE VEAU
BRILLAT-SAVARIN

4 freshly made thin pancakes, about 7 inches
  across
4 escalopes of veal (each roughly 4 oz.)
5 tablespoons butter
salt and pepper
12 button mushrooms, sliced thin
2½ teaspoons chopped shallots
⅓ cup dry sherry
5 tablespoons grated Gruyère cheese

METHOD: Sauté the veal in 3 tablespoons butter until nicely browned and very nearly cooked—about 8 minutes. Season, remove from pan, and keep hot. Sauté mushrooms and shallots in the same butter. Add the sherry, season, and cook, stirring constantly, until the sherry is reduced. Place 1 teaspoon mushroom-and-shallot mixture on one half of each pancake; put on this a nearly cooked escalope, cover with more shallot mixture, and then fold pancake over so that it makes an envelope. Arrange in a buttered dish. Place ½ tablespoon butter on each and sprinkle with the grated cheese. Put under broiler to finish off; brown nicely. Serve at once. Serves 4.

ESCALOPES DE VEAU AUX CONCOMBRES

> 4 escalopes of veal
> 4 tablespoons butter
> 1 cucumber
> salt and pepper
> ⅔ cup cream
> paprika

METHOD: Pound escalopes well to make them as thin as possible. Sauté in 3 tablespoons butter until browned on each side. Remove from pan and keep hot.

For the cooking of the cucumber there are two schools of thought: either simply to boil it in salted water, or to cook it in very little water and butter, the idea being that a cucumber contains a great deal of water and will in cooking yield a sufficient quantity for stewing in its own juice, so to speak. Both methods are satisfactory, but the cucumber cooked in water seems to taste fresher and cooler and is more of a contrast to the rich cream sauce. In either case, peel the cucumber first, and when it is done cut it in slices 1 inch thick. Keep hot.

In the pan in which the escalopes have cooked, there will be coagulated juices of the meat sticking to the sides and bottom. Scrape these well with a fork and add cream, a pinch of paprika, and salt and pepper. Stir well and bring to the boil. Keep boiling briskly for a few minutes, stirring until the sauce is the consistency of thick cream. Add 1 tablespoon butter, a small piece at a time, over very low heat. Place the escalopes and the pieces of cucumber in a serving dish and pour the sauce over them. Serves 4.

This recipe was given to me by Monsieur Jean Paul, like Raymond a chef on the *Train Bleu*. How I used to wish that lady chefs could be employed on those famous trains, but they never were. All my life I have wanted to travel; except once, when I went for the day to Boulogne, I never have been able to. Now I see Miss Godden set off for the Continent or the East or America—particularly America— and I ache to go with her, but I'm always left behind to look after those scamps of Pekingese.

POT-AU-FEU

> 2 lbs. lean beef rump
> 1 small cabbage
> 2 carrots
> 1 parsnip
> 2 leeks
> 1 turnip
> 1 onion
> bouquet garni (see index)
> 12 cloves
> 10 peppercorns
> 1¼ teaspoon salt
> 1 loaf stale French bread

METHOD: Tie beef into a good round shape with string. Put into a heavy iron or flameproof earthenware pot with 3 to 4 quarts water. Bring to the boil and skim. Clean and cut vegetables into medium-sized pieces; cut the cabbage into quarters. Tie the bouquet garni up, along with the cloves and peppercorns, in a piece of cheesecloth. Put all into the pot with the beef, add salt, and simmer gently for 4 hours.

Remove the bouquet garni. Cut French bread into slices and put into a soup tureen. Lift out the vegetables carefully and lay them on the bread. Put the meat on a separate dish, pour the broth into the tureen, and serve. The meat should be served separately; tomato sauce (see index) may be poured round it. Serves 6.

BEEF OLIVES

1 small onion
6 small mushrooms
¼ cup minced ham
½ teaspoon chopped parsley
½ teaspoon grated lemon rind
¼ cup breadcrumbs
½ teaspoon thyme
salt and pepper
1 egg, beaten
8 slices beef rump, ¼ inch thick
4 tablespoons butter
1¼ cups stock
⅔ cup white wine
1 heaping tablespoon flour

METHOD: Preheat oven to 350°. Chop onion and mushrooms finely and mix with the ham, parsley, lemon rind, breadcrumbs, and thyme. Season with salt and pepper; add beaten egg. Put some of this mixture on each slice of beef. Roll up the slices and secure with thread. Melt 2 tablespoons butter in a casserole and brown the beef rolls in it. Add stock and wine, cover, and simmer gently in oven for 1 hour; turn the rolls from time to time.

Remove beef rolls from oven, cut away thread, and put them into a hot serving dish. Melt 2 tablespoons butter in a pan, stir in the flour, and gradually add the gravy from the casserole; stir until bubbling. Pour the sauce over the beef olives and serve. Serves 8.

Despite its name, this dish contains no olives. The "beef olives" are the beef rolls.

STEAK AND KIDNEY PUDDING

> 1 cup chopped suet
> 1¾ cups flour
> ½ teaspoon salt
> 1½ lbs. lean chuck steak
> ½ lb. beef kidney
> ½ cup flour, seasoned with salt and pepper,
>   for dredging
> ½ cup sliced mushrooms
> 1 onion, chopped
> ⅔ cup stock or water

METHOD: Blend the suet, flour, and salt to a paste and line a greased 2-quart pudding basin * with it, keeping a little paste for the top. Cut the beef into chunks, trimming off fat and gristle. Cut up the kidney, discarding centre core. Dredge beef and kidney in seasoned flour. Into the lined bowl place alternating layers of meat, mushrooms, and onion. Add stock or water and cover with the remaining paste. Cover the pudding with a sheet of greaseproof paper and on top of that lay a muslin or cotton cloth about 2 feet square. Secure these by tying a length of string tightly around the rim of the bowl. The hanging ends of the cloth may then be drawn together and tied in a knot on the top. Fill a large kettle with water to within 2 inches of the top. Bring to a boil, place the bowl in the kettle, cover, and steam for 4 hours. (Fresh boiling water should be kept handy to replenish the kettle as water boils away.) Then leave the pudding in the kettle, off the heat, for a day. Steam again for 1½ hours. Serve in the bowl with a table napkin pinned around it. A jug of beef gravy should accompany it. Serves 6.

FILLET OF BEEF WITH MAÎTRE D'HÔTEL BUTTER

> 4 tablespoons butter
> 1 tablespoon chopped parsley
> 1 teaspoon lemon juice
> pepper to taste

* Pyrex or ovenproof china casserole, shaped like a mixing bowl, with rimmed edge.

> 4 4- to 6-oz. slices of beef fillet, ½ inch thick
> 1 clove garlic, cut
> 1 tablespoon oil
> ⅓ cup white wine
> ½ teaspoon chopped parsley
> ¼ teaspoon thyme

METHOD: Put butter on a flat saucer; knead with a blunt knife until malleable. Mix in 1 tablespoon parsley, lemon juice, and pepper, and turn and turn again until the butter has absorbed all the moisture. Wet the hands in cold water and shape the butter into a small roll. Put into the refrigerator until hard.

Remove all fat and any gristle from the fillets; rub both sides with garlic. Mix oil, wine, ½ teaspoon parsley, and thyme, and marinate fillets in this in a deep dish for 2 hours. Turn the fillets at least three times. Remove them from marinade and put under a hot broiler. Time them according to the liking of the eater, that is: 3 minutes on each side for rare; 4 to 5 minutes on each side for medium rare; 8 minutes on each side for well done.

Cut the butter into four pieces and put one on top of each fillet. This is a far quicker method than making each pat separately. Serves 4.

VIENNA STEAKS

> 2 shallots
> 1½ lbs. lean chopped beef
> salt and pepper
> 1 egg, separated
> breadcrumbs
> oil
> watercress

METHOD: Chop the shallots, mix with the beef and seasonings, mix in egg white, and form into six neat patties. Beat egg yolk, dip patties into it, and roll them in breadcrumbs. Sauté in hot oil for 10 minutes, turning once. Serve hot, with sprigs of watercress. Serves 4 to 6.

BEEF IN WINE

> 2½ to 3 lbs. rump steak
> 6 slices fatty bacon
> salt and pepper
> 1 onion
> 1 teaspoon mixed herbs (see index)
> ⅔ cup sherry
> ½ lb. button mushrooms, caps only

METHOD: Preheat oven to 350°. Cut beef into neat slices. Place bacon at the bottom of a flameproof casserole and heat through on a low flame. Season beef well with salt and pepper, and add. Chop the onion finely and add to the casserole with the herbs. Add sherry, cover, and bake in oven for 3 hours. Twenty minutes before time is up, add the mushrooms. Serves 6.

This is my own version of the famous Burgundian dish Boeuf Bourguignon, which is good served with red wine from that region.

OXTAIL STEW

> ½ lb. dried lima beans
> 2 onions
> 1 turnip
> 2 carrots
> 1 stick celery
> 3 lbs. oxtails
> 2 tablespoons butter
> 1 teaspoon mixed herbs (see index)
> 1 bay leaf
> salt and pepper to taste
> ⅓ cup flour
> ⅓ cup port wine

METHOD: This recipe needs to be started four days before the stew is to be eaten. On the first day, soak the beans in cold water overnight. The next day, peel and slice the vegetables and sauté them with the oxtails in butter in a large heavy-bottomed pan. Add 2½ quarts water, herbs, and seasoning. Drain the beans and add them. Bring to the boil, skim, and simmer, partially covered, for 3 to 4 hours. Leave until thoroughly cold. Remove the fat from the top of the stew.

On the third day, bring to the boil and then simmer again for 3 to 4 hours. Leave to get cold and remove fat. On the fourth day, bring to the boil and simmer again for 3 to 4 hours. Leave to get cold and remove fat and large bones. Reheat. Mix flour to a paste with a little water and stir into the stew until it thickens. Before serving add port wine; this greatly enhances the flavour. Serves 6 to 8.

When I was in that first of all posts as the least of least housemaids in Kensington Square, oxtail stew was always given to us in the servants' hall on Wednesday evenings, a hot redolent stew, plus mashed potatoes fried to a golden brown. How good it was! It's true that, growing as I was and working hard under termagant Amy, I was always ravenous, but the dish is good, fit for a king. (I have served it to a prince.) In Kensington Square I liked it so much that, in spite of Amy, I snooped until I found out how it was made, asking discreet questions of the scullery maids and kitchenmaids, praising their work until I was able to keep in my mind the various ingredients and the—to me, then—complicated method. Later on I often cooked this stew and, when I was in command, used my imagination, as I always say cooks must, and added extras. For instance, the Kensington Square stew had no port wine; my oxtail stew became even better than that one.

JUGGED NECK OF LAMB

3 tablespoons butter
2 onions, quartered
3 lbs. best end neck of lamb
4 small tomatoes
1 stick celery
salt and pepper
1¼ tablespoons flour
1¼ cups stock
1¼ tablespoons lemon juice
2½ tablespoons red-currant jelly
1 tablespoon chopped parsley
⅓ cup port wine

METHOD: Preheat oven to 350°. Melt 1 tablespoon butter in a stew pan and brown the onions. Cut lamb into pieces, trim off fat, and brown in pan with onions. Peel tomatoes, chop celery, and put into a greased casserole. Add meat and onions and season. Melt 2 tablespoons butter, stir in flour and brown it, stir in stock over medium heat, continue stirring until it thickens, and add lemon juice. Pour the sauce over the meat, cover, and bake in oven for 2 hours. Add the redcurrant jelly, chopped parsley, and port, 10 minutes before serving. Serve very hot in casserole. Serves 6.

LAMB BRETON

2½ tablespoons oil
2 lbs. boneless lamb from the leg
4 medium onions
3 slices bacon, diced
1 clove garlic, chopped
¼ lb. mushrooms, sliced
salt and pepper
2 teaspoons flour
1 tablespoon tomato purée
⅔ cup red wine
1¼ cups stock
1 tablespoon sherry
bouquet garni (see index)

METHOD: Preheat oven to 350°. Heat the oil in a large heavy-bottomed pan; add lamb and brown it carefully all over. Remove and keep warm. Slice onions and add to the same oil with the bacon, garlic, and mushrooms. Season and cook slowly for 4 to 5 minutes. Shake in the flour and brown, stirring constantly. Add the tomato purée, red wine, sherry, stock, and seasoning. Stir over heat until the sauce boils. Put in the lamb with the bouquet garni. Cover pan tightly and bake in oven for 50 minutes. Take out lamb, keep warm. Reduce the gravy in the pan to the consistency of cream and serve separately. Serves 6.

BAKED LAMB CHOPS

12 small or 6 large lamb chops
1 large onion
salt
pepper
1 heaping tablespoon flour
1¼ cups meat stock

METHOD: Preheat oven to 350°. Remove excess fat from each chop, reserving fat. Place chops in a circle in a greased baking pan. Slice the onion fine and lay slices over the chops; season with salt and pepper. Now cover with the fat trimmings and bake in oven for 1 hour. From time to time, turn the chops and be sure that the slices of onion have not burnt.

When done, remove chops and onions and place in a hot serving dish.

Drain off the fat and discard the trimmings. Put the pan over medium heat on top of the stove. With a wooden spoon, stir the flour into the baking pan, mixing well into the juices round the sides. Now gradually add the stock and keep stirring until it boils well. If this sauce is too pale, add a few drops of gravy colouring. Pour over the chops and serve. Serves 6.

Pork chops may be used in the same way, with a little grated sour apple put into the sauce.

I had often thought, when serving plain broiled lamb chops, what a lot of the chop was left uneaten—broiled fat is peculiarly unappetizing—so I thought I would have a try at cooking chops in a way of my own. It was really an inspiration, and I can say that whenever I send this dish to table the chops are eaten down to the bone.

BENGAL CURRY

1 lb. lamb from leg or shoulder
2 small onions
3 cloves garlic
2 small tomatoes
oil or fat for frying
½ teaspoon grated fresh ginger, or 1 teaspoon
   dry ground ginger
½ teaspoon ground turmeric
1 teaspoon ground cumin
1 heaping teaspoon ground coriander
½ teaspoon chili powder (optional)
1 cup hot water

METHOD: Cut lamb into pieces 1½ inches square; chop onions; chop garlic very fine; cut tomatoes into small pieces. Heat oil or fat on moderate heat in a large heavy-bottomed pan and, when sizzling hot, add onions, garlic, and ginger (if fresh). Sauté for 1 or 2 minutes, add pieces of lamb, and increase the heat to make it quite hot, so as to prevent too much juice of the meat coming out. Sauté until the meat is a rich brown, stirring constantly; then lower the heat to moderate and add turmeric, cumin, coriander, ginger powder (if fresh ginger is not used), and chili powder if desired. Sauté 2 minutes. Add the tomatoes and sauté another 2 minutes. Then add hot water and let it come to the boil. Lower heat, cover the pan, and let simmer on *very* low heat. Stir, off and on, to prevent sticking. The meat should take 45 minutes to become tender. The gravy should be thick and not watery. Serves 2.

PORK CHOPS WITH TURNIPS

6 large pork chops or 12 small ones
2½ tablespoons clarified pork dripping
1½ lbs. small white turnips
salt and pepper
2½ cups hot water or stock

METHOD: Preheat oven to 325°. Brown the chops in dripping in a flameproof casserole. Remove and keep warm on a hot plate. Then peel the turnips and cut them in half and brown in the same fat. Replace chops at bottom of casserole with turnips on top. Season. Add enough hot water or stock to half cover, and boil for 10 minutes. Then let simmer for 40 minutes in oven. Correct seasoning and arrange chops on a hot serving dish with the turnips around them. Serves 6.

PORK FRANCINE

> 3 onions
> 4 small tomatoes
> 3 lbs. good lean pork
> 2 tablespoons butter
> ¼ cup tomato purée
> bouquet garni (see index)
> 1 teaspoon paprika
> ⅔ cup white wine
> 2½ teaspoons red-currant jelly
> ⅔ cup stock
> salt and pepper

METHOD: Chop the onions, peel and quarter the tomatoes, and cut the pork into cubes. Sauté the onions in a large heavy-bottomed pan in the butter until nice and brown, then stir in the pork. Do not brown this. Cover the pan and cook over low heat for 15 minutes, shaking the pan occasionally.

Now add the tomatoes, tomato purée, bouquet garni, paprika, wine, red-currant jelly, and stock. Season with salt and pepper. Simmer over low heat for 2½ hours. Serves 6.

This truly excellent dish once landed me in quite a tizzy. I was working, at the time, for a cosmopolitan household where many different people used to come to dinner. My employer was a very busy woman who gave me a free hand to make up my menus, saying there was no need to consult or bother anyone.

One night for a party I decided to serve the Pork Francine and had the dish well under way, in fact there was not much time to go until dinner must be served, when the butler, who had been putting finishing touches to the table, came in.

"What's that lovely smell?"

I told him, and dismay came over his face. His was noth-ing to *my* dismay when he told me the guests that night were Jewish and "completely frum" (strictly Orthodox). Luckily I had a large fillet of steak in the refrigerator and was able to serve quite another kind of dish in time, but I did regret my Pork Francine.

BAKED GAMMON

> 4-5 *lbs. gammon (smoked ham)*
> *short pastry made with 6 cups flour, and water*
> *(see index)*
> 1¼ *cups breadcrumbs browned in butter*

METHOD: Soak ham in water to cover for 2 hours. Preheat oven to 350°. Wipe ham dry and trim off brown pieces. Cover all over with short pastry. Put the ham on a rack in a roasting pan, cover with buttered paper, and bake for 2 hours. When cooked, remove the crust and skin, cover with browned breadcrumbs, and serve either hot or cold. Serves 12. Pease pudding is delicious with this dish.

PEASE PUDDING

> 1 *lb. split peas*
> *salt and pepper*
> 2 *tablespoons butter*

METHOD: Soak peas overnight in water to cover. Drain and wash well. Put into pan, cover with cold water, and add 1 teaspoon salt. Bring to a boil and simmer very, very gently until peas have become thoroughly soft and mushy, about 2½ hours. Remove from heat, beat well with a wooden spoon, taste for salt, and add a little pepper and the butter. Stir well and serve. Serves 12.

QUICHE LORRAINE

> 2 *cups self-raising flour*
> ½ *teaspoon salt*
> 4 *tablespoons lard*
> 4 *tablespoons butter*

6 slices bacon (*streaky will do*)
3 eggs
2 cups heavy cream
¼ teaspoon nutmeg
salt and pepper

METHOD: For pastry, sift flour and ½ teaspoon salt, put into a mixing bowl, put in lard and butter cut into tiny pieces, pour in ⅓ cup water, and mix lightly with a knife into a firm dry dough. Roll it out and line a flan tin (not too shallow). Store in a cool place until ready for use. Preheat oven to 375°.

For filling, cook bacon until crisp, drain, and break into small pieces. Break eggs into bowl, add cream, nutmeg, salt, and pepper, and beat until well mixed. Arrange bacon over pastry, pour egg mixture over it, and bake for 35 to 40 minutes. Serves 4. Serve with a crisp green salad.

POULTRY AND GAME

POULET MARENGO

½ lb. mushrooms
7 tablespoons oil
1 3- to 4-lb. chicken
10 small onions, peeled
2 cloves garlic, chopped
1 heaping teaspoon flour
⅓ cup red wine
2 cups stock
4 small tomatoes
1 teaspoon tomato purée
bouquet garni (see index)
1 teaspoon paprika

2 bay leaves
salt and pepper
8 large or medium shrimp
4 eggs
croûtons of brown bread (see index)
chopped parsley

METHOD: Preheat oven to 350°. Peel and stem the mushrooms, chop peelings and stems, and reserve. Heat 4 tablespoons oil in a large flameproof casserole and brown the chicken, turning it on one side, then the other. Remove chicken and put in the onions, chopped garlic, and chopped stems and peelings of the mushrooms. Sauté for 5 minutes. Take pan off heat, stir in the flour, and pour in the wine and stock. Cut up two tomatoes and add these to the pan together with the purée. Bring to the boil, replace chicken, add the bouquet garni, paprika, and bay leaves. Season, cover the pan, braise in oven 30 to 40 minutes, or until chicken is tender.

For garnish, quarter the mushrooms; skin, quarter, and seed the other two tomatoes. Remove the shells from the tails only of the shrimp, leaving on the heads and claws, and warm them in a little butter. Fry the eggs in 3 tablespoons oil. Keep hot. Strain the gravy from the chicken into another pan; add the mushrooms to it and simmer while cutting the chicken into serving pieces. Put chicken and quartered tomatoes into the pan with the sauce. Reseason and simmer with the lid off for about 5 minutes. Take out chicken and arrange on hot serving dish. Pour sauce carefully over chicken. Place eggs at either end of the dish with the shrimp. Evenly arrange croûtons in centre. Scatter chopped parsley over all. Serves 4.

POULET BRAISÉ AU RIZ

4 tablespoons butter
1 onion
3 slices bacon, cut in small pieces
1 4-lb. chicken
1¼ cups stock
⅓ cup sherry
1½ tablespoons flour
3 cups braised rice (see index)

METHOD: Preheat oven to 350°. Put 1 tablespoon butter in a stew pan large enough to hold the whole chicken. Peel and slice onion and sauté until nice and brown. Add bacon and sauté together a minute or so longer. Put chicken in with these and sauté it until it is brown all over, turning it first on one side, then on the other. Add stock and sherry, cover, and put into oven to simmer gently for 1½ hours or until chicken is tender.

When done, remove chicken, keep hot, strain liquid, and remove all fat. Melt 3 tablespoons butter, stir in flour, mix well, and gradually add the chicken liquid, stirring, making sure you do not let the sauce get too thin. Cut chicken into portions and arrange these on a hot serving dish. Pour the sauce over them and make a border of rice. Serves 4 to 6.

BRAISED RICE

> 1 cup Patna rice, or Carolina long-grain
> 1 thin slice bacon or lean ham
> 2 shallots
> 3 tablespoons butter
> ½ teaspoon mixed herbs (see index)
> salt and pepper
> 2 cups stock

METHOD: Preheat oven to 350°. Wash rice, drain well; chop bacon or ham, and the shallots. Melt butter in a pan and sauté the shallots and bacon or ham to a golden brown. Add mixed herbs, salt, and pepper. Add the rice and stir over heat until it all looks golden. Now add stock, completely covering rice. Put the lid on the pan and bake in oven for 45 minutes. Remove from oven and stir with a fork. Serves 4 to 6.

POULET LOUISETTE

> 2 teaspoons oil
> 4 tablespoons butter
> 1 4-lb. roasting chicken cut up
> 1 onion
> 2 cloves garlic
> 1 heaping tablespoon flour
> ⅔ cup white wine
> 1¼ cups chicken stock
> bouquet garni (see index)
> ½ cucumber, peeled and sliced
> 2 thin slices cooked ham
> 6 mushrooms
> 1 teaspoon mixed herbs (see index)
> salt and pepper
> 2 egg yolks
> 4 tablespoons cream
> baked crescents of puff pastry (see index)

METHOD: In a heavy-bottomed pan large enough to hold the chicken pieces, heat the oil and 2 tablespoons butter. Place the chicken in this and brown it all over. Remove the chicken and keep hot. Chop the onions, crush the garlic, and add to the pan. Sauté for a few minutes, add the flour, stir well, then pour on the wine and stock. Bring to a boil, replace the chicken, add the bouquet garni, and simmer for ½ hour.

Meanwhile melt 2 tablespoons butter in a pan and add peeled and sliced cucumber. Cover and cook for 4 to 5 minutes. Chop the ham, slice the mushrooms, and add to cucumber with the herbs. Season and simmer for 2 to 3 minutes.

Remove bouquet garni from the chicken and pour stock from the chicken onto the cucumber mixture.

Stir the egg yolks well with the cream and add this to the stock. Sir over low heat until the sauce thickens, mixing carefully.

Pour this sauce over the chicken. Arrange all in a hot serving dish with hot puff pastry crescents set round the edges. Serves 4 to 6.

CHICKEN WITH PAPRIKA

1 5-lb. pullet
2 onions, peeled
8 tomatoes
½ teaspoon dried tarragon
¼ cup clarified dripping (preferably pork)
a few bacon rinds
2 tablespoons butter
2 tablespoons flour
½ cup milk
½ cup stock from chicken
1 tablespoon paprika
salt and pepper

METHOD: Preheat oven to 425°. Stuff the bird with one onion, two of the tomatoes, and the dried tarragon. Put it into a deep casserole with half of the dripping. Cut the second onion into rings and add. Prick the skins of six tomatoes with a knife and add. Cover with bacon rinds and the rest of the dripping. Put on lid and bake in oven for 10 minutes; then reduce heat to 350° and bake slowly for 2 hours, basting occasionally. When done, remove chicken from pan and allow the stock to cool, keeping the chicken warm. When the stock is cold, remove all fat from it. Then cut up the chicken and reheat in the stock. Remove the chicken pieces and again keep them hot while the sauce is made.

Melt the butter, stir in the flour, add milk and stock and stir over heat until thick. Add paprika and salt and pepper. Cook for a few minutes and pour this sauce over the chicken. Serves 4 to 6.

POULET AUX ASPERGES

1 3-lb. chicken, cut up
2 onions
2 carrots
bouquet garni (see index)
1 teaspoon dried savoury
2 teaspoons chopped parsley
⅓ cup white wine
2½ cups chicken stock

> 1 clove garlic, crushed
> 1 tablespoon gelatine
> 1 teaspoon salt
> ½ teaspoon pepper
> 1 12-oz. tin asparagus spears, or ½ lb. fresh
>   asparagus, cooked

METHOD: Preheat oven to 350°. Place the chicken in a roasting pan. Slice the onions and carrots and add with the bouquet garni, savoury, parsley, wine, stock, and garlic. Cover with oiled or buttered greaseproof paper. Bake 1½ hours or until tender. Remove chicken from pan and cool.

Dissolve gelatine in 2 tablespoons stock. Strain the remaining hot stock and return to pan. Add the melted gelatine, stirring well to dissolve every particle. Season with salt and pepper. Line the bottom of a tureen or loaf-shaped pan with some of the asparagus. Pour over this a little of the prepared stock and put in refrigerator to set. Remove chicken flesh from bones and cut into neat pieces. When first layer is set, fill pan with alternating layers of chicken and asparagus. Pour the remaining stock over all. Cover with foil and place a weight on top. Chill thoroughly. Remove from pan, slice if desired, and serve with salad. Serves 4.

CHICKEN RISOTTO

> 5 tablespoons butter
> 1 medium-sized onion
> 1 carrot
> ¼ lb. mushrooms
> 2 tomatoes
> 1 stick celery
> 1 clove garlic
> 2½ tablespoons chopped ham
> 2 cups cut-up cooked chicken meat
> ⅓ cup dry white wine
> salt and pepper
> 2 teaspoons chopped parsley
> 3⅔ cups chicken stock
> 1½ cups long-grain rice
> 2 tablespoons grated Parmesan cheese

METHOD: Heat 2 tablespoons butter in a large skillet which can be covered. Slice the onion and carrot and sauté slowly for 5 minutes. Meanwhile, slice the mushrooms, peel and chop the tomatoes into small pieces, slice the celery, and crush the garlic. Add to the pan and cook for 2 minutes more. Stir in the ham and chicken and add the wine. Increase the heat so the dish cooks fast for a couple more minutes; add seasonings and parsley and stir in ⅔ cup stock. Cover the pan and cook slowly for ½ hour.

In a saucepan, bring the remaining stock to a boil and add the rice. Cover the pan and simmer slowly for about 15 minutes, until the liquid is absorbed and the rice is tender. Put the rice and the chicken mixture in a serving dish. Stir in the 3 tablespoons butter and sprinkle with grated cheese. Serves 6.

CHICKEN PILAU

1 4-lb. chicken
1 teaspoon salt
½ teaspoon pepper
2 medium-sized onions
4 tablespoons butter
½ cup seedless raisins
¼ cup split blanched almonds
1 cup long-grained rice
2 cups chicken stock
salt and pepper

METHOD: Season the chicken pieces with 1 teaspoon salt and ½ teaspoon pepper and cook in a steamer until tender (about 1 hour).* Slice the onions and brown lightly in 2 tablespoons butter; add ¼ cup raisins and cook 2 or 3 minutes more. Add the almonds and continue cooking until they are golden brown. Remove all from pan and keep warm.

Melt remaining 2 tablespoons butter in a saucepan and gently sauté the rice until it is golden, about 5 minutes. Add the stock and the rest of the raisins; simmer gently, covered, for 20 minutes or until the liquid is absorbed and the rice is tender. Season to taste. Serve on a hot dish with chicken piled

* If you prefer the chicken browned, the pieces may be seasoned and sautéed in a covered frying pan in 4 tablespoons butter and oil for about ½ hour, or until the chicken is tender.

in the centre, rice surrounding it, and the onions, raisins, and almonds scattered on top. Serves 4.

POULET MIREPOIX

> 10 tablespoons butter
> salt and pepper
> bouquet garni (see index)
> 1 4-lb. roasting chicken
> ⅓ cup white wine
> 2 leeks
> 2 carrots
> 1 onion or 2 shallots
> 1 small turnip, peeled
> 1 clove garlic
> ¼ cup green beans
> 1 12-oz. tin celery hearts, drained
> 1 lb. peas, shelled
> 2½ tablespoons cream
> 1 teaspoon mixed herbs (see index)
> ¾ lb. grapes, peeled and seeded

METHOD: Preheat oven to 350°. Put 3 tablespoons butter, salt and pepper, and bouquet garni inside the bird. Smear 3 tablespoons butter over the breast, put the chicken in a roasting pan with the wine and 1¼ cups water, cover with foil, and roast in oven for 1½ hours, basting frequently. Fifteen minutes before the chicken is cooked, remove foil.

Prepare the mirepoix. Clean and chop leeks, carrots, onion, and turnip. Crush garlic. Melt in a fairly large pan 4 tablespoons butter. Add the cleaned and chopped vegetables together with the beans, celery hearts, and peas; season with salt and pepper. Mix well, cover tightly, and simmer over low heat for 30 to 40 minutes, shaking pan occasionally.

Remove chicken from oven, carve it, and arrange pieces in a ring in a large shallow flameproof dish. Put the vegetables in the centre of the dish and keep all hot. Reduce the gravy in the roasting pan and, off heat, add the cream. Whisk this well and add the mixed herbs and grapes. Pour over the chicken. Serves 4.

Poulet mirepoix, which was shown me by Marcel, is one of the most delightful in this book. It needs patience, especially in peeling the grapes—always a niggling job—but the colours of the different vegetables with the chicken really make it look like a painting. As for the smell—"fragrance" is a better word—it always brings Rumer Godden straight down to the kitchen. *Poulet mirepoix* is easily her favourite dish.

CHICKEN CASSEROLE

2 tablespoons butter
1 carrot
1 onion
1 stick celery
1 5-lb. boiling fowl, cut up
¼ lb. mushrooms
1½ cups stock
1 tablespoons tomato purée
salt and pepper
1 teaspoon chopped parsley

METHOD: Heat the butter in a large pan. Peel and slice carrot and onion, chop the celery, and sauté them for a few minutes. Add the chicken and brown on each side. Slice the mushrooms and add with the stock and tomato purée; season and cover pan. Simmer gently for 2 hours, or until tender. Add more stock if necessary. Sprinkle with chopped parsley. Serves 4 to 6.

PIGEON WITH PEAS

4 tablespoons butter
1 onion
4 pigeons
salt and pepper
boiling stock to cover
2 teaspoons tomato purée
1 lb. new green peas
1 teaspoon basil

METHOD: Melt butter in a deep pan. Chop the onion, add it with the pigeons, and brown them all over. Season and add enough boiling stock to cover the birds. Stir in the tomato purée. Cover and simmer gently 1½ hours, then remove pigeons and keep hot. Shell the peas and cook in the liquid the pigeons have cooked in for 20 minutes. Replace pigeons, allow to cook another 5 minutes, add the basil. Turn all out into a hot dish and serve. Serves 4.

Once, in a country post, I had an Italian boy as my kitchen helper. He was forever going out into the woods in the early afternoon with a gun he had borrowed, and would come back with a pigeon or two, which he would coax me to cook for him when they had hung. I got so tired of the wretched things roasted plain that I made up my own recipe for this interesting dish. The Italian boy said, "*Molto buono,*" and I think it is.

FAISAN À LA CRÈME

4 tablespoons butter
1 pheasant
2 onions, chopped
2 teaspoons flour
⅔ cup cream

METHOD: Melt butter in a deep pan and sauté the pheasant with the chopped onions. Cover and simmer slowly until the bird is quite tender, about 1 hour. Remove bird and carve. Put meat into a casserole. Strain the juice the pheasant was cooked in and return it to the pan. Mix the flour with a little water, stir into the sauce, and cook to thicken. Add the cream. Pour this sauce over the bird and keep very hot until served. Serves 3.

CASSEROLE OF PHEASANT

1 large pheasant, cut up
2 tablespoons butter
2½ tablespoons oil
6 shallots, peeled
½ teaspoon thyme
salt and pepper
⅓ cup brandy
1¼ cups cream

METHOD: Preheat oven to 325°. Put pheasant into a casserole with the butter and oil, shallots (whole), thyme, salt, and pepper. Cover pan and put into oven for 1½ hours. After 1 hour add the brandy; 15 minutes later stir in the cream. Arrange the pieces of pheasant on a platter with shallots around them; pour the sauce over the dish, and serve. Serves 4.

GUINEA FOWL AU PORTO

2 cloves garlic
1 teaspoon each, rosemary and savoury
2 3-oz. packages cream cheese
2 guinea fowl
4 tablespoons butter
salt and pepper
2 tablespoons cognac
⅓ cup port wine
4 shallots
2 tablespoons oil
truffles, or truffle peelings, or 8 button
    mushrooms
1 tablespoon cream

METHOD: Preheat oven to 350°. Pound the garlic with the herbs, then beat into the cheese. Divide cheese in half and put one half into each bird. Melt butter in baking pan, put in the birds, and brown quickly; now put them into the oven, add salt and pepper, and roast for 1 hour. After 45 minutes, pour in the cognac and light it. When flame has died down, pour in half the port and baste frequently.

While the birds are cooking, peel and slice shallots. Brown them in oil and simmer over low heat for just a few minutes. Season and add truffles or truffle peelings, and their juice (or the mushrooms); simmer again for 5 minutes. Heat up the rest of the port and pour this over the shallots and truffle peelings; simmer very gently for 10 to 25 minutes. At the last moment, stir in the cream. Carve the fowl, arrange on a hot dish, and pour sauce over. Serves 4.

PERDRIX AUX CHOUX

1 good-sized Savoy cabbage
salt and pepper
6 small partridges
3 tablespoons butter
2 slices fat bacon
2 teaspoons flour
1¼ cups stock
bouquet garni (see index)
6 small link sausages

METHOD: Clean cabbage, cut into quarters, and put to soak in cold water for 5 minutes. Drain and salt it slightly. Put partridges in a casserole with butter; season and add the bacon. Brown the birds over moderate heat, then add flour, stirring it in well into the butter. Add stock and the bouquet garni. Cover casserole and simmer briskly for 20 minutes.

In the meantime cook the cabbage in a little boiling water and drain. Brown the sausages until done and add to the casserole with the cabbage. Re-cover the casserole and simmer very gently until the partridges are cooked, about another 15 to 20 minutes. Serves 6.

PERDREAUX PROVENÇALES

2 good-sized partridges
2 thin slices bacon
4 tablespoons butter
1 clove garlic, cut in half
¼ lb. mushrooms
⅓ cup white wine, preferably Chablis

METHOD: Preheat oven to 350°. Wrap the partridges in bacon, put into a heavy-bottomed casserole with butter, and add the garlic. Cover with buttered greaseproof paper. Bake in oven for 1 hour. Ten minutes before the time is up, remove the paper. Remove the birds and keep them hot. Slice mushrooms and sauté in the same butter on the top of the stove. Add wine, bring to a boil, stir well, and reduce a little.

A few minutes before serving, remove the garlic and discard. Put the partridges in the casserole again and simmer over low heat with the lid on, to warm thoroughly. Serve in the casserole. Serves 4.

It was my old friend Raymond again who showed me how he did this dish—but showed me with reluctance, as he said he did not like anyone, even me, "poaching on his preserves." It was not until I had lost touch with him, many years later, that I dared to cook it, and I never do without thinking about him.

VEGETABLES

LYONNAISE POTATOES

12 small potatoes
salt
2 small onions
1 cup (½ lb.) butter
2 teaspoons chopped parsley

METHOD: Wash potatoes well but do not peel. Put into salted boiling water and cook until tender but unbroken, about 20 minutes. Remove skins while hot and slice into thick slices. While potatoes are cooking, slice onion fine and sauté in 2 tablespoons butter to a golden brown.

Put the rest of the butter in a pan that is large enough to

hold all the potato slices. Melt the butter and drop the slices into this; increase heat and sauté so that they are brown and crisp all over. Remove from heat, sprinkle lightly with salt, add the onions, mix well, and sprinkle with chopped parsley. Serves 6.

DUCHESSE POTATOES

4 to 6 medium potatoes
1 teaspoon salt
4 tablespoons butter
2½ tablespoons milk or thin cream
pepper to taste
1 egg

METHOD: Peel potatoes and cut into pieces. Put into saucepan, cover with water, add the salt, and boil until very tender, about 20 minutes. Drain thoroughly and put back on low heat for a couple of minutes to dry out.

Put the potatoes through a sieve, using a wooden spoon to press them through it into an empty dry pan. With the same spoon, beat in the butter, milk, and pepper. Beat the egg and add to the potato. Stir very briskly until the mixture is light and fluffy. Butter an ovenproof serving dish, spoon potatoes into this; smooth them down, then rough up with a fork. Place under medium-hot broiler until golden brown. Serves 4.

POTATO PANCAKES

4 large potatoes
2 medium-sized onions
2½ tablespoons plain flour
salt and pepper
oil

METHOD: Peel and grate raw potatoes and drain off any surplus liquid. Grate the onions. Into a bowl put the grated potatoes, grated onions, flour, and seasoning. Mix this well. Heat a little oil in a frying pan—it must be very hot— and drop a tablespoon of the mixture at a time into the oil.

Cook until golden brown on both sides. Drain well. Keep all hot and serve. Serves 4.

SPINACH

> 1 *lb. young spinach*
> *salt and pepper*
> *2 tablespoons butter*

METHOD: Wash spinach well in several changes of water; remove stalks. Lift the spinach with the hands, shaking it well, and place in a saucepan just large enough to hold all the leaves without the addition of further water.

Sprinkle salt and pepper over spinach, cover, and cook over low heat 8 to 10 minutes, pressing the mass down from time to time with a wooden spoon. Drain well, put into a hot dish, and dot with butter. Serves 4.

SPINACH LEAVES IN JAPANESE TEMPURA

> 1 *lb. very fresh spinach*
> *1 egg yolk*
> *⅔ cup ice water*
> *¾ cup flour*
> *salt and pepper*
> *oil for deep-frying*

METHOD: Use the smallest spinach leaves whole and break larger ones into equal pieces. Wash these and dry carefully to avoid bruising. To make the tempura, beat egg yolks and water together. Sift flour and salt and pepper and gradually add (using a spoon), stirring *lightly* from bottom of mixing bowl. The flour should not be too well mixed in. Ignore lumps. Heat deep oil until it is very hot. (Test by dropping a piece of bread into it; if the oil is hot enough, the bread will immediately rise to the top.) Dip leaves in the batter and then drop them, a few at a time, into the hot oil. When coloured and crisp, remove with tongs and drain on a cloth or paper. Keep very hot and serve. Serves 4 to 6.

Small lettuce leaves, mushrooms, and cauliflower flowerets can be done in the same way.

SPINACH PARMESAN

> 1 lb. spinach
> 4 tablespoons butter
> salt and pepper
> ½ teaspoon nutmeg
> 2 heaping tablespoons grated Parmesan cheese

METHOD: Cook spinach as directed on page 133. Drain well. Place the spinach in a pan with the butter; season and add a pinch of nutmeg. Allow butter to melt, then stir in the grated cheese and serve hot. Serves 4.

YOUNG BROAD BEANS IN PODS

> 2 lbs. unshelled young broad (or lima) beans
> 1 teaspoon salt
> 2 tablespoons butter

METHOD: Use very small broad beans about 2 to 3 inches long, gathered before the "fur" is formed inside the pods. Remove tips at both ends. Fill a large pan with water, add salt, and when it is boiling put in the bean pods and cook a good 10 minutes. Drain, add the butter, shake well, and place in serving dish. Serves 4.

These are delicious cooked in the way I do them, but I have had many a battle with gardeners over asking for such tiny beans. I have been told not to "go prowling about the kitchen garden"; it was not my business. "My lovely beans," they used to say, "murdered, taken up to the house for 'her' to do 'em in.'" Gardeners usually hate being asked for small and young vegetables; they want their vegetables to grow to a huge size and don't seem to care that they lose all taste and are tough. [Mrs. Manders has converted Mr. Manders, however; and the most tender of infant beans, peas, marrows, and turnips arrive from his garden in the cornucopia basket.—R.G.]

HULLED BROAD BEANS

2 lbs. broad beans
1 teaspoon salt
1 tablespoon butter
1¼ teaspoons flour
2 teaspoons milk
2 teaspoons cream
1 tablespoon chopped parsley

METHOD: Shell the beans and wash well. Bring salted water to a boil in a saucepan. Add beans and cook until the skins have separated from the beans (about 10 minutes). Drain and keep pan warm until it is required for the finished beans. Now carefully remove the outer skin from each bean. When all are skinned, put the beans back into the pan to keep warm. Melt the butter in a small pan, stir in the flour, and mix well over medium heat. Stir in the milk and cream. Let this sauce cook until it bubbles (it can be thinned with a little of the bean water). Add the chopped parsley, stir again, and pour over the beans. Reheat gently and put into a serving dish. Serves 4.

RATATOUILLE

1 red and 1 green pepper
2 small eggplants or 1 large one (about ¾ lb.)
4 small tomatoes
1½ cups sliced onions
6 to 8 tablespoons olive oil
1 teaspoon salt
½ teaspoon pepper

METHOD: Cut up peppers; remove seeds. Cut unpeeled eggplant into large cubes; skin and chop tomatoes.

Sauté onions in oil for a few minutes, add peppers and eggplant, and continue cooking 6 to 8 minutes. Add tomatoes, salt, and pepper. Cover pan and simmer gently for 20 to 25 minutes, stirring occasionally. Vegetables should not be too mushy, so to evaporate excess liquid remove lid and boil fast for a few minutes longer, stirring occasionally to avoid sticking. Serve in very hot ramekins or ovenproof dishes. Serves 6 to 8.

SALSIFY

> 4 salsify roots
> 2 teaspoons salt
> 2 teaspoons lemon juice
> 2 tablespoons butter
> 2 tablespoons flour
> 1 cup water from cooking salsify

METHOD: Wash and peel the roots, keeping them under water to preserve the colour. Rinse in cold water with 1 teaspoon each salt and lemon juice. Put into boiling water with 1 teaspoon salt and 1 teaspoon lemon juice and boil for 10 minutes or until soft. Drain and keep hot. Now melt butter, stir in flour, and gradually stir in 1 cup salsify stock. Stir over heat until sauce thickens. Arrange salsify in a dish, pour the sauce over, and serve. Serves 4.

This vegetable can also be dried after cooking, cut into half-lengths, dipped into a good batter, and fried in deep oil.

CELERIAC SANDWICHES

> 2 lbs. celeriac
> salt
> ½ cup tomato purée
> 1 teaspoon ground ginger
> 2 eggs
> 2 cups breadcrumbs
> oil for frying

METHOD: Peel celeriac and cook in boiling salted water about 20 minutes. Drain and cool and cut in thick slices. Mix tomato purée with a little salt and the ground ginger. Spread on one slice of celeriac and cover with another. Continue this until all the slices are sandwiched. Beat the eggs, dip each sandwich in them, and dredge it in breadcrumbs. Fry in deep hot oil (375°) 5 to 10 minutes. Serve very hot. Serves 4 to 6.

[I had not met celeriac before Mrs. Manders came to us. It makes a most unusual dish; the flavour is so delicate that we often serve it as a separate course. I myself like it best simply cut into slices and boiled, then served with a velouté sauce—i.e., a white sauce flavoured with the celeriac water. —R.G.]

COURGETTES*

> 12 very small courgettes
> salt and pepper
> ½ cup grated cheese
> 4 tablespoons butter
> 1 tablespoon chopped parsley

METHOD: Choose courgettes not more than 3 inches long. Wipe well but do not peel. Cook whole in boiling salted water for 15 minutes. Drain and cut into thick slices. Butter an ovenproof dish (or individual dishes). Place slices in this, season lightly, sprinkle with the grated cheese. Cut the butter into small dice and dot over all. Put under broiler until brown. Sprinkle the whole with chopped parsley and serve. Serves 6.

STUFFED AUBERGINES†

> 1½ tablespoons long-grained rice
> salt and pepper
> 3 aubergines
> 2 tomatoes
> 2 red peppers
> oil for deep frying
> ½ teaspoon paprika
> pinch of saffron

METHOD: Cook the rice in boiling salted water for 20 minutes. Cut the aubergines in two lengthwise and sprinkle with salt to bring out some of the water. Leave for 10 minutes. Skin and chop tomatoes; chop peppers. Wipe aubergines dry and deep-fry in hot oil (375°) until done—roughly 7 minutes. Remove and drain. Scoop out the flesh and chop it in a bowl; add the cooked rice, tomatoes, and red peppers. Season with salt, pepper, paprika, and saffron. Stuff the aubergines with this mixture and brown under the broiler. Serves 6.

* Zucchini.
† Eggplants.

AUBERGINES* WITH WINE SAUCE

> 2 medium-sized aubergines
> 2 tablespoons butter
> 2 small onions
> ½ cup breadcrumbs
> 1 teaspoon chopped parsley
> 2 egg yolks
> 1 teaspoon salt
> freshly ground pepper
> 4 teaspoons butter
> wine sauce (see index)

METHOD: Preheat oven to 350°. Parboil the auber-gines in boiling salted water until tender but not soft, about 7 minutes, depending on size; test with a fork to be sure. Cut them in half lengthwise and scrape the flesh out into a bowl, being careful not to break the skin. Chop the flesh. Melt 2 tablespoons butter in a pan; chop the onions finely and brown them lightly in the butter. Remove from heat and mix with the aubergine flesh, crumbs, parsley, egg yolks, salt, and a dusting of pepper. Mix well, then refill shells. Put these into a well-buttered flameproof serving dish; put 1 teaspoon butter on top of each aubergine half and bake in oven for ½ hour, or until browned. Serve with wine sauce. Serves 4.

WINE SAUCE

> 1 very thin strip lemon peel
> juice of 1 lemon
> 1 tablespoon sugar
> pinch of salt
> ½ teaspoon paprika
> 1 teaspoon arrowroot
> 2 tablespoons butter
> 1 tablespoon brandy
> ⅓ cup dry sherry

METHOD: Put the strip of lemon peel into a pan with ⅓ cup water and the lemon juice and simmer for 5

* Eggplants.

minutes. Remove peel, add sugar, salt, and paprika. Mix the arrowroot with 1 tablespoon cold water. Put lemon-juice mixture over heat. When it is boiling, stir in the prepared arrowroot. Add the butter in small pieces. Mix well and off heat add the brandy and sherry. Serve hot. Makes about 1 cup.

BRUSSELS SPROUTS WITH CHESTNUTS

> 1 lb. Brussels sprouts
> ½ lb. chestnuts
> salt and pepper
> 6 tablespoons butter
> 1¼ tablespoons flour
> 1¼ tablespoons brown sugar
> water in which sprouts have cooked

METHOD: Preheat oven to 350°. Clean sprouts. Cut a slit in the pointed end of each chestnut and boil for 10 minutes; then peel and boil them in salted water until tender —approximately a further ½ hour. Cook sprouts in boiling salted water 15 minutes. Drain, reserving 1¼ cups of the water. Heat the butter in a small pan; add the flour and brown it. Stir in the sugar and mix well. Add slowly the reserved sprout water and stir until the sauce thickens. Mix the chestnuts and sprouts together and pour the sauce over them. Place in a hot serving dish and put into oven until heated right through, about 15 minutes. Serves 4.

CASSEROLE AUX CHOUX

> 1 large white cabbage
> salt and pepper
> ⅛ lb. salt pork
> 1 onion
> 2 tablespoons butter
> 1 peppercorn
> 2 cloves
> ⅓ cup white wine
> a little stock or water
> ¾ lb. streaky bacon
> 1 tablespoon chopped chives

METHOD: Thoroughly wash, clean, and quarter the cabbage. Blanch it in slightly salted boiling water for 7 minutes. Remove, drain, and shred. Cut the rind from the salt pork and put into a casserole. Chop the onion finely and add with the butter, peppercorn, and cloves. Add the shredded cabbage, the wine, and enough water or stock to cover. Bring to the boil, then simmer gently for 1½ hours. Add the streaky bacon and cook for 1 hour more. Arrange in a hot serving dish and garnish with chopped chives. Serves 6.

ENDIVE

6 *heads endive*
salt and pepper
2½ *cups stock*
½ *teaspoon sugar*
1 *heaping tablespoon flour*
2½ *tablespoons milk*
2 *tablespoons butter*
1¼ *tablespoons lemon juice*

METHOD: Wash endive thoroughly and put into boiling salted water. Simmer 10 minutes, then drain and chop finely. Put into a pan with the stock and sugar. Simmer for 10 minutes more or until tender. Drain endive. Mix the flour with the milk and stir into the stock. Add the butter, stir well until bubbling, and add the endive. Reheat, add lemon juice, and season to taste. Put into a hot serving dish. Serves 4 to 6.

SALADE DE RIZ

1 *cup long-grained rice*
1 *lb. prawns (large shrimp)*
½ *lb. peas, shelled*
salt to taste
1¼ *cups mayonnaise (see index)*

METHOD: Cook rice, unshelled prawns, and peas separately in boiling salted water until tender. Reserve six to eight of the best prawns for garnishing and shell the rest. Drain the rice and peas and put aside to cool. Then put them in a salad bowl with the shelled prawns. Add mayonnaise and mix thoroughly. Garnish with the remaining prawns. Serves 4.

CRAB SALAD

> 1 large crab, cooked *
> salt and pepper
> parsley to garnish

METHOD: Clean crab: Remove dead men (the grey excrescences on the shell). Pull purse away from shell. With a picker, remove bead or coral and put it into a bowl. Break purse with small hammer and remove all white meat, carefully avoiding any pieces of shell. Put meat into another bowl. Remove claws and legs, break them, carefully pick out the white meat, and put into the bowl with the other meat. From the stripped shell, remove any coral or brown substance and put into the bowl containing the other coral. Season the contents of each bowl with a little salt and pepper and mash each separately with a fork. See that the empty shell is nice and clean and break away the outside rim, which has a mask all the way round. Now pack the white flesh into each side of the shell; press down so that it all goes in. In the centre of this, press in the coral or bead. Arrange small parsley bunches in a row down each side of the centre filling. Serves 4 to 6.

[When Mrs. Manders finds something outstanding that, as she says, "simply asks to be cooked" (she means by herself), she is apt to get so excited about it that it becomes the most important thing, at that moment, in the world. Crab salad always reminds me of an evening last spring when, as usual in the evening, I was in my study, deep in the writing of a novel and far, far away from home or anyone real, in the atmosphere of an imaginary monastery I was trying to create.

Suddenly there was a loud knock at the door and Mrs. Manders burst in—"burst" is the only word—her face flushed, eyes blazing with excitement. "Look! What a beauty!" And down on my table, on and among my pages

* Dungeness crabs are appropriate for this dish.

and notes and books, she plopped an open cardboard box from which waved two enormous pinkish-apricot things like claws or pincers. "Isn't it a beauty—straight off the boat!"

"But what *is* it?" Mrs. Manders must have thought me "wanting," but I was still not really back.

"What is it? It's a crab. The biggest, finest crab I've ever seen, and fresh. Mr. Manders has just been down to the quay—the boats are in—and he brought this up. Shall we have it?"

"*Not* on my novel," I wanted to cry, "and not under my nose." But there was the crab, waving its claws—she was right, it was outsize—and edging and moving in the box, while there she stood, exulting.

There was nothing else to do but laugh.—R.G.]

SWEETS

PRUNE MOULD

1 *lb. dried prunes*
6 *tablespoons sugar*
1 *tablespoon gelatine*
grated rind of ½ lemon

METHOD: Soak prunes overnight in water to cover. Simmer them in 1 cup water with the sugar until tender. Rub through a sieve. Soak gelatine a few minutes in ½ cup water. Dissolve it in ½ cup hot water and strain into the prune pulp. Add lemon rind, mix well, and pour into a mould to set. Chill. Turn out onto a dish and serve with cream. Serves 4 to 6.

When I was with "Madam" at Cowes—my pretty gay lady—I had to make prune mould three times a week because she used to have it, minus the cream, every morning with camomile tea, and nothing else. I began to hate the very sight of a prune, but she bloomed on this strange breakfast; it certainly kept her face and figure perfect.

CRÊPES SUZETTE

1 cup flour
salt
2 teaspoons finely granulated sugar
1 egg
1 egg yolk
⅔ cup milk
1 tablespoon brandy
2 teaspoons melted butter, cooled
4 lumps sugar
1 large orange
5-6 tablespoons butter
3 tablespoons finely granulated sugar
1 tablespoon Curaçao or Grand Marnier
2 tablespoons lemon juice
extra sugar
2-3 tablespoons brandy, warmed

METHOD: Make the batter for the pancakes well beforehand. Sift flour with pinch of salt into a bowl, stir in 2 teaspoons sugar, make a well in the centre, and drop the egg and egg yolk in. Gradually add ⅔ cup water to make a smooth batter; beat well. Add the milk and beat hard until bubbly. Leave to stand for 4 hours if you can. Before using, beat again and stir in the brandy and melted butter. The batter now should be the consistency of thin cream. If too thick, add a little more milk.

Before cooking the pancakes, make the sauce in the following way. Rub the sugar lumps over the skin of the orange until they are well soaked with its aromatic oil. Squeeze the orange and strain the juice. Put the sugar lumps into a chafing dish or a large frying pan with the butter, 3 tablespoons sugar, the strained juice of the orange, and the Curaçao. Now turn to the pancakes.

Heat a small omelette pan well and, for the first pancake, add a very little butter, just enough to make the pan shiny; probably none will be needed for the rest. The pancakes must be very thin and light, so pour only a little batter into the pan for each, tilt this way and that until it covers the pan surface evenly, and cook over a good heat, shaking the pan gently. When surface of the pancake begins to bubble, turn it and cook it on the other side. Sprinkle each pancake with a little lemon juice and keep aside in a warm place until all are done.

Now put the pan containing the sauce on the heat and, as soon as it starts bubbling, put in the first pancake. When it is well cooked, fold it in four, right side out—that is, the side that touched the pan first and is the most attractively speckled. Put in the next pancake, and proceed as before. When all are folded, slide them and turn them in the sauce until they are piping hot and have absorbed as much of the sauce as possible. Just before serving, sprinkle a little sugar over the crêpes and put them quickly on a hot dish. At table, pour over them the warmed brandy and set alight. Serves 6 to 8.

GÉNOISE

> 4 eggs
> ½ cup finely granulated sugar
> 1 scant cup confectioner's sugar
> ½ cup (¼ lb.) butter, melted
> ⅓ cup rum or brandy
> flavourings (4 oz. melted chocolate, a few
>   drops orange extract, or, if liqueurs are
>   used in the crème, omit flavourings)
> ½ cup sugar
> 4 egg yolks, beaten
> ½ cup (¼ lb.) unsalted butter
> flavourings (melted chocolate, orange extract,
>   Curaçao, Grand Marnier, Maraschino, or
>   Kirsch)
> chopped almonds
> ⅓ cup chopped pistachio nuts

METHOD: This is a sweet rather like a cake, very rich, with a cream filling. Preheat oven to 300°. In a warmed bowl, beat the four whole eggs well, then beat with ½ cup finely granulated sugar. Beat this until it thickens to the consistency of mayonnaise. Add, little by little, the confectioner's sugar, melted butter, rum or brandy, and flavoring, if used. The mixing bowl should be hot when these ingredients are put in, so do this at the side of a warm oven if possible. Line a square or round pan, fairly deep, with greaseproof paper, well buttered and sprinkled with flour. Pour in batter and bake for 45 minutes.

For the crème, boil ½ cup sugar in 3 tablespoons water until it has reached the first stage; that is, when it has become syrupy but has not turned to a pale caramel. Remove from heat. Add, little by little, the egg yolks, stir well, and let the mixture cool. Then add butter (which *must* be unsalted), working it well in with a wooden spoon. Lastly add the flavouring. Be sure that the crème is smooth.

Cut the Génoise horizontally in half, sprinkle both pieces well with liqueur or brandy or rum, according to what goes best with the crème. Put a thick layer of crème between the two halves of the cake. Coat sides and top with crème, and cover well with chopped almonds and pistachio nuts. Serves 8 to 10.

CHOCOLATE MARIE

> 4 oz. semisweet chocolate
> 1¼ tablespoons light Karo syrup
> 4 eggs, separated
> ⅔ cup cream, whipped
> Maraschino cherries

METHOD: Melt chocolate in the syrup over hot water. Remove from heat and add egg yolks. Stir well. Beat the egg whites until stiff and fold them in. Arrange in glasses and decorate with whipped cream and cherries. Put into refrigerator to set. Serves 4 to 6.

Funnily enough, whenever I make this sweet my memory goes back to a post I held for a while at a large country seat, one of the most beautiful places you can imagine. It was summer, and on a warm June or July evening the windows would be open and as I melted chocolate or folded in whites of eggs in the evening quietness, my every sense seemed gratified: the sight of the dining table laid in all its glory; the smooth touch of the fine bone-china plates and dishes my kitchenmaid was putting to warm; the smell coming in through the window of the roses in the garden; the sound of birds singing and, faint, of a tune being played in the drawing-room. The tune? "In the Still of the Night." And not least, the taste of this delectable dish. Whenever I make it the memories come back.

PEACH MERINGUE PORCUPINES

> 4 ripe fresh peaches
> 1 tablespoon Kirsch
> 3 egg whites
> salt
> ¾ cup sugar
> 8 almonds, blanched and cut into thin slivers

METHOD: Put peaches into boiling water for 1 minute; cool and skin. Put them on a heatproof serving dish, make a small incision on top of each one, and fill with a few drops of Kirsch.

Preheat oven to 350°. Beat egg whites with a pinch of salt and ¼ cup sugar until sticky. Now add the remainder of the sugar and continue beating until mixture stands up in peaks. Using a knife and tablespoon, cover each peach with the meringue mixture, making sharp, pointed little peaks with the knife. Stick almond slivers round each peach until it is covered with spikes. Put into oven for 10 to 15 minutes, watching carefully until the porcupines are a good beige colour. Serve with cream. Serves 4.

PEACH CUSTARD

> 2 large peaches
> sugar to taste
> ½ cup rice flour (or cornstarch)
> 2½ cups milk
> ¼ cup ground almonds
> 2 eggs

METHOD: Halve, stone, and peel the peaches; poach them in ½ cup water for a few minutes. Add sugar and allow to cool. Preheat oven to 350°.

Mix the rice flour to a paste with a little of the milk. Bring the rest of the milk to a boil in a pan, stir gradually into rice paste, and add the almonds, mixing well. Sugar to taste. Now beat the eggs well and add. Put into a round fireproof dish and bake for ½ hour. Mash the stewed peaches to a pulp, spread this over the top of the custard, and serve. Serves 4.

If fresh fruit is unobtainable, use several tablespoonfuls of peach jam.

FONTAINEBLEAU MELON

> 1 large cantaloupe
> 2½ tablespoons Kirsch
> sugar to taste
> 3 3-oz. packages cream cheese
> 2½ tablespoons cream

METHOD: Cut a cap off the stalk end of the melon and scoop out all seeds. With a spoon, scoop out all the flesh in curls the size of a walnut and put them in a bowl with the Kirsch and a little sugar. Leave for 1½ hours. Beat the cheese and cream together until smooth, stir in more sugar to taste, stir in the melon and any juice left in the shell. Put all back into the shell and serve cold. Serves 6.

ORANGE CARAMEL

> 5 navel oranges
> 2 tablespoons finely granulated sugar
> 4 tablespoons Sauternes
> ¼ cup granulated sugar
> ⅔ cup hot water
> ⅔ cup whipped cream

METHOD: Peel oranges, divide into sections, remove all pith, and arrange sections in a glass bowl. Sprinkle with finely granulated sugar and the Sauternes.

Put the granulated sugar in a saucepan and melt it slowly. Cook until dark brown, but do not burn. Add the hot water, mix, and cook until a thick caramel is formed. Pour this onto a buttered plate to harden, then break it into little pieces and sprinkle over the orange. Decorate top with the whipped cream. Serves 6.

SOUFFLÉ AU SABAYON

> 3 eggs, separated
> 6 tablespoons sugar
> juice of 2 lemons and grated rind of 1
> 3 drops vanilla extract
> 2 cups sweet white wine
> 1 tablespoon gelatine
> 1 cup whipped cream
> a few crystallized violets for decorating

METHOD: Whisk egg yolks, sugar, lemon juice, and vanilla in a bowl over boiling water until thick and light. Add lemon rind and cool. Warm the wine, dissolve the gelatine in it, and whip until cool. Whip the cream. Beat egg whites until stiff. Add gelatine to the cooled yolk mixture, fold in ⅔ cup cream, then fold in egg whites. The mixture should set almost at once, so fill a soufflé dish quickly. Decorate with rosettes of whipped cream round the edges; put a ring of crushed crystallized violets on top. Chill. Serves 6.

CHOCOLATE SOUFFLÉ

> 2 oz. semisweet chocolate
> ⅔ cup milk
> 3 eggs, separated
> 6 tablespoons sugar
> 2 ozs. French almond rock (barley sugar
>   sprinkled with a little almond extract can
>   be substituted)
> ¼ teaspoon vanilla extract
> ⅓ cup sweet white wine
> 1 tablespoon gelatine
> 1¼ cups cream

METHOD: Melt chocolate in milk over hot water. Whisk egg yolks, sugar, and the chocolate in a bowl over boiling water until thick and light. Pound the rock or barley sugar and add to the mixture with vanilla extract. Warm the wine, dissolve the gelatine in it, and add. Whip the cream. Beat the egg whites until stiff. Fold these in and pour into a soufflé dish. Chill. Serves 6.

CRÈME BRÛLÉE

> 3 egg yolks
> 2 tablespoons finely granulated sugar
> 1¼ cups light cream
> ¾ cup granulated sugar
> 1 teaspoon syrup glucose *

METHOD: Beat egg yolks with the finely granulated sugar in a bowl until the sugar is absorbed. Heat the cream (but do not boil) in a pan over water and pour very gradually over the yolks, stirring constantly. Return all to pan. Continue stirring over water on low heat until the mixture thickens; do not let it boil. Pour into a serving dish and refrigerate to set for 6 hours.

Then prepare the caramel. Put the granulated sugar, together with the glucose and 4 tablespoons water, into a pan. Stir over low heat until light brown. Turn out the custard onto a plate and coat with the caramel. Put back into refrigerator for another 5 minutes. Spread another thin layer of caramel on the top and serve. Serves 4.

STUFFED ORANGES

> 2 oranges
> 1 apple, chopped
> 2 teaspoons raisins
> 2 teaspoons grated nuts
> 2 teaspoons sugar
> ⅓ cup whipped cream

METHOD: Cut oranges in half, remove seeds, and scoop out the flesh. Mix the orange flesh, apple, raisins, and grated nuts. Add sugar. Heap this mixture into the halved oranges. Top with whipped cream. Serves 4.

* This can be bought at a drugstore. It is simply liquid glucose.

MARRONS SUPREME

> 1¼ cups toasted almonds
> 6 tablespoons butter
> 1 lb. marrons glacés (or a tin of vanilla-
> flavoured crème de marrons)
> 1 tablespoon almond liqueur

METHOD: Chop the almonds. Cream the butter and in another bowl beat the marrons thoroughly with a wooden spoon. Beat the butter into the marrons; then add three-quarters of the almonds, and the liqueur. Pile all this onto a serving dish. Chill. Just before serving sprinkle with the remaining almonds. Serves 6.

POUDING CHOCOLATE ITALIE

> 4 egg yolks
> 4 tablespoons sugar
> 4 tablespoons butter
> 10 tablespoons grated semisweet chocolate
> 1 teaspoon Maraschino
> milk
> 24 ladyfingers

METHOD: Beat egg yolks and sugar together. Melt the butter, let it cool, then pour gradually into the sugar and eggs, stirring all the time. Add the chocolate and mix well together over low heat until chocolate is melted. Mix the Maraschino with a little milk and soak the ladyfingers in it. Line a 1-quart charlotte mould with these. Pour the mixture in and cover with more ladyfingers. Put into the refrigerator until set. Turn out and serve. Serves 6.

VIENNESE TORTE

> 3 eggs, separated
> 1¼ cups sugar
> 1½ cups almonds
> 1 tablespoon red-currant jelly

METHOD: Preheat oven to 350°. Beat egg yolks with ½ cup sugar until pale and honey-coloured. Blanch, peel, and mince the almonds; stir half of these into the yolks.

Choose a cake pan with removable sides, butter it well, and put mixture in it. Bake ½ hour, or until crisp. Beat egg whites until stiff and add remaining sugar and almonds. Remove sides of cake pan and cool slightly. Spread top with red-currant jelly, then cover with the egg whites. Put back in oven and bake 10 minutes or until pale brown. Serves 4.

CUSTARD

> 2½ cups milk
> 6 tablespoons sugar
> 1 vanilla bean
> 3 eggs

METHOD: Put milk, sugar, and vanilla bean into the top of a double boiler. Put pan over hot water on low heat. Whisk the eggs, add them, and stir until the mixture thickens. (As it is in a double boiler it will not boil, which would make it curdle.) Remove vanilla bean and pour custard into custard glasses. Serves 4 to 6.

Custard has now an unusual connection in my mind.

My son, Warwick, was on HMS *Eagle*, and in May 1964 an invitation came for me to attend the Recommissioning Ceremony and have luncheon on board. How I looked forward to this great honour!

On a lovely May morning I set off, dressed to the nines in a new black suit, with a black patent-leather handbag and new nylon stockings and smart black suede shoes. My son had told me to wait for him inside Devonport Dockyard, but when I arrived, the naval police told me none of the crew was allowed off the ship, so I went with other guests in a bus to where the *Eagle* was tied up.

We were escorted on board and taken down in the lift to the enormous hangar, now emptied of planes and brightly decorated with bunting; at one end was a big dais draped with the Union Jack and the good old white ensign. There were hundreds of chairs set out in rows, and the whole ship's complement, 2500 men, were at the back. I found myself seated in the first row. My goodness! There was gold braid to right of me, gold braid to left, and a great deal of what my father used to call "custard on the cap" (custard again!). I tried to pick out Warwick, but it was useless in that sea of faces.

The skipper, Captain D. Empson, read the Commissioning Warrant from the dais and gave the Gaelic Blessing. There were prayers and a hymn, "Eternal Father, strong to save." Then the Naval Prayer was said by everyone, and the Captain addressed the Ship's Company and guests. "God Save the Queen" was sung. It was all deeply moving and impressive, and I had a big lump in my throat. Then Lady Henderson, wife of the Commander-in-Chief (Plymouth), cut the Commissioning Cake.

When the ceremonial part was over, we were taken up by lifts to the flight deck. Everyone was in family groups, and as they disappeared to see over the ship I was left feeling most forlorn. I paced the deck until the Royal Marines band arrived to play "Every Nice Girl Loves a Sailor," marching up and down. At last a young officer came to my help, and the next thing I heard was a voice over the loudspeaker saying plainly, "Will Mrs. Manders go to the quarterdeck, where her son is waiting for her."

Warwick was like a thundercloud. "Where have you been? Why didn't you wait for me?" I explained what the police had told me. But he had been ashore all the time!

However, we both recovered and I had my tour of the ship. He took me up and down ladders till I was breathless, showing me everything, clambering and climbing; but of course to me most interesting of all were the galleys. Everything was beautifully clean, spick-and-span, and my eyes at once lighted on a gigantic cauldron of—guess—custard. I had never imagined so much could be made at once. It was destined for serving with the fruit salad at the sumptuous luncheons that were laid on in the various messes: our dining room had two thousand guests. There was a choice of three hot dishes, or a cold one. In a smaller room, tables were set out with every kind of cheese. Coffee followed. Everything was beautifully cooked and served, and we were waited on like royalty. After this generous repast, we took our departure.

I felt thoroughly tired after the miles I had walked; my feet were swelling in the smart shoes, my nylons were ruined, but never mind. Warwick suggested we should take a trip by bus over Dartmoor, a perfect ending for a lovely day and one I shan't forget as long as I live—and I'll never forget that custard.

SAVOURIES

[Savouries—those tasty little tidbits—used to come at the end of a full-scale dinner, separating the sweet or pudding course from dessert.

In America, "dessert" is used, I know, to designate the sweet course itself, but in England it denotes something quite else. The sweet course, of pudding, mousse, ice, fruit salads, and so on, was followed immediately by the savoury, which ended the dinner proper. The table was then cleared, crumbs were swept, the cloth was drawn or table-mats were removed, and special dessert plates, usually of fine china, were set before the guests; on each plate would be a fine doily and a finger bowl, the water slightly warm, made fragrant by one or two flowers or leaves such as sweet geranium or lemon verbena; there would also be fine silver, or perhaps silver and ivory or silver and mother-of-pearl, dessert knives and forks.

Then, on the table, small silver or china dishes of nuts, dried fruit, crystallized fruit, bonbons, and chocolates would be set, together with a tall dish, perhaps pedestal-footed, piled high with fruit. Decanters of port or madeira would be set before the master, the requisite glasses having been put at each place. The decanters were never lifted but pushed from place to place, which is why they were placed in "coasters"—round silver or Sheffield-plate holders, the bases of rounded polished wood covered with felt, so as not to scratch the table.

Often the older children of the house would come down to dessert, dressed in party clothes, and were given a few sweets or nuts and perhaps a thimbleful of the wine. After a short while the hostess would "catch the eye" of the chief woman guest—sometimes difficult if she was talking—and the ladies would rise and withdraw, leaving the gentlemen to their wine. It is from this "withdrawing" that we have the word "drawing-room"; it was the "withdrawing room" where presently the gentlemen would join the ladies for coffee and liqueurs.

The salty or savoury taste of the savouries was, I suppose, to separate the sweet course from those of the "dessert" (the English have not as sweet a tooth as the Americans). Savouries were also, I think, a preparation for the port and madeira—often very fine wines.—R.G.]

TOMATO SAVOURY

> 1 small onion
> 1 cup canned tomatoes
> 2½ teaspoons chutney
> pinch of paprika
> 1 bay leaf
> ½ cup grated Cheddar cheese
> 1 teaspoon Worcestershire sauce
> 1 teaspoon salt
> 3 eggs
> 4 rounds of brown bread
> 2 tablespoons butter

METHOD: Chop onion finely, drain and cut up tomatoes; if chutney has large pieces, chop these. Mix these ingredients with the paprika, bay leaf, cheese, Worcestershire sauce, and salt, in a pan. Break the eggs into a bowl and stir but do not beat; add eggs to mixture and heat until it thickens, but remove before it boils, or the eggs will curdle. Fry rounds of brown bread to golden brown in butter and spread the mixture on them. Remove bay leaf before serving. Serves 4.

CHEESE RAMEKINS

> ½ lb. short pastry (see index)
> 3 eggs
> 2 cups milk or cream
> salt and pepper
> ½ lb. Cheddar cheese, grated

METHOD: Preheat oven to 350°. Line six greased individual ramekin dishes with pastry. Beat the eggs and milk and seasoning together; add the cheese and fill the dishes three-quarters full. Bake for 20 minutes. Serves 6.

CRÊPE NIÇOISE

> ½ cup flour
> 1 egg
> 1 egg yolk
> 1 tablespoon oil
> salt and pepper
> ⅔ cup milk
> 2 hard-cooked eggs
> 4 tablespoons butter
> ¼ cup chopped mushrooms
> 2 teaspoons flour
> ⅔ cup stock
> 2 cups minced cooked chicken or ham
> 1 tablespoon chopped parsley
> 2 teaspoons cream
> ¼ cup grated Cheddar cheese

METHOD: For the pancakes, put ½ cup flour into mixing bowl with 1 egg, 1 egg yolk, oil, and ½ teaspoon salt. Beat until smooth and add milk. Continue beating until mixture is like cream; add a little more milk if too thick. Leave in a cool place for 2 hours.

Shell hard-cooked eggs and chop finely. Melt 2 tablespoons butter in a pan, add mushrooms, season, cover, and cook slowly for 3 to 4 minutes. Remove from the heat and stir in 2 teaspoons flour and stock; then bring back to the boil, add meat and hard-cooked eggs, parsley and cream. Heat omelette pan and brush it with a little oil. Cover bottom with a thin coating of the pancake batter; brown one side, then the other; remove pancake and keep hot. Cook the rest of the batter in the same way. Put a spoonful of the filling in the centre of each pancake, fold over, and arrange in heatproof dish. Melt 2 tablespoons butter, pour over crêpes, and sprinkle with grated cheese. Brown under broiler. Serves 4 to 6.

CHESTNUT CROQUETTES

> 2 lbs. chestnuts
> 2 shallots or 1 small onion, chopped

½ cup (¼ lb.) butter
salt and pepper
3 eggs
2 cups breadcrumbs
fat for deep frying

METHOD: Prick chestnuts and boil them for ½ hour or until tender. Shell, peel, and mash them with the shallots. Melt the butter and add. Season with salt and pepper. Beat 2 eggs lightly and add. Mix all together. Form into croquettes. Beat the third egg. Dip the croquettes in egg and breadcrumbs. Fry in deep hot fat (375°) until golden. Serve with hot tomato sauce (see index) or stewed tomatoes. Serves 6.

Christmas and chestnuts always seem to me to go together: chestnut stuffing for the turkey, and marrons glacés —especially those made by Madame Floris in Brewer Street, Soho, which seem far more delicious than any others. But chestnuts also give me a memory that is really nostalgic. In my younger days I was a great "first-nighter" and, whenever I had a post in London, used to watch the theatre news. When a first night was announced I used to go along to the theatre, hire a camp stool, and take my place in the queue for the pit. Lone wolf as I was, usually I went alone, and I can remember how frightened I was as I walked home after seeing Russell Thorndyke in the Grand Guignol series in St. Martin's Lane. In winter, sitting on the camp stool perhaps for hours, one got terribly cold, and walking back in excitement—sometimes in fear—was colder still. Then what a comfort it was to buy a bag of hot lovely-smelling chestnuts from the chestnut man with his glowing brazier! Many and many a time have I done this, warming not only my hands but my inners, right down to the cockles.

TOMATO SAUCE

1½ tablespoons butter
4 small tomatoes
2 teaspoons chopped onion
½ teaspoon sugar
1¼ cups well-flavoured stock
1 small bay leaf
2 tablespoons flour
1 teaspoon lemon juice
salt and pepper

METHOD: Melt the butter in a large heavy-bottomed pan. Wipe the tomatoes and slice into the pan with the butter. Add the onion and sauté gently for 10 minutes. Add the sugar, half the stock, and the bay leaf. Blend remainder of the stock with the flour and stir this into the pan; add the lemon juice and pepper and salt to taste. Cover and let all simmer gently for ½ hour. Remove from heat and rub through a fine hair sieve. Put back into a pan to reheat, and serve. Makes about 3 cups.

CHEESE FRITTERS

3 eggs
2½ tablespoons flour
1 lb. Cheddar cheese
salt and pepper
paprika
2 cups dry cracker crumbs
fat for deep frying

METHOD: Beat eggs and mix with the flour to form a smooth batter. Grate the cheese, add, and mix well. Season with salt, pepper, and a little paprika. Shape mixture into small balls; roll in cracker crumbs. Fry in hot deep fat (375°) until brown. Serves 6. Serve hot with green salad.

CHEESE AND TOMATO TOAST

> 1 medium-sized tomato
> 1 tablespoon butter
> 1 tablespoon grated Cheddar cheese
> 2 eggs, beaten
> salt and pepper
> 4 rounds of bread, toasted and buttered

METHOD: Peel and slice the tomato. Melt butter in a pan, add tomato, sauté until cooked. Add the cheese and beaten eggs and stir over low heat until the mixture thickens. Season, pour over rounds of hot buttered toast, and serve. Serves 4.

CHEESE CUSTARD

> 1 cup grated Cheddar cheese
> 1 cup breadcrumbs
> 1 egg
> 1¼ cups milk
> salt and pepper

METHOD: Preheat oven to 350°. Grease a 1-quart flameproof dish. Mix cheese and breadcrumbs in a bowl. Beat the egg in another bowl, add milk, and pour over the cheese and breadcrumbs. Season to taste. Pour into greased dish and bake for ½ hour. Serve hot. Serves 4.

CHEESE PUDDING

> 1 cup grated Cheddar cheese
> a little chutney
> 6 thin slices bread
> 1 tablespoon butter
> 2 eggs
> 2 cups milk
> salt and pepper
> ¼ lb. ham scraps

METHOD: Grease a 1½-quart flameproof dish. Preheat oven to 350°. Mix ¾ cup cheese with a little chutney. Trim away the crusts from the slices of bread and butter them. Make sandwiches of these with the cheese and chutney as filling. Cut sandwiches in half and arrange in the greased dish. Whisk together eggs, milk, and seasoning. Arrange ham over the bread slices and pour the milk mixture over them. Sprinkle the rest of the cheese on the top and bake for ½ hour. Serves 6.

CHEESE RISOTTO

4 slices bacon
1 onion
2 tablespoons oil
1 cup long-grained rice
2½ cups stock, heated
4 mushrooms
1 tablespoon butter
1 cup grated cheese

METHOD: Chop bacon and onion. Heat oil in a shallow pan, add rice, bacon, and onion, and sauté gently for 2 to 3 minutes, stirring well. Stir in hot stock and bring to a boil. Lower heat, cover, and simmer for 20 minutes, or until rice is tender and the liquid has evaporated.

Sauté the mushrooms in the butter. When the rice is cooked, fold in the mushrooms and half the grated cheese. Put the risotto in a hot serving dish, sprinkle with remaining cheese, and serve. Serves 6.

CANAPÉ À L'ESPAGNOLE

6 croûtes (see index)
4 tablespoons cream cheese
1 cup mayonnaise (see index)
pinch of paprika
2 teaspoons chopped pimiento, or 1 tablespoon anchovy paste mixed with 6 tablespoons butter, plus yolk of 1 hard-cooked egg

METHOD: Spread the croûtes thinly with cream cheese. Flavour mayonnaise with paprika and pipe through a pastry bag, around the edges of the croûtes. Decorate each in the centre with a tiny heap of minced pimiento. Or you may spread the croûtes with anchovy paste creamed with butter, and decorate each with a little heap of chopped egg yolk in the centre.

Serve the croûtes on separate dishes, or make both varieties and serve, arranged alternately, on a silver dish. Serves 6.

INDIAN EGGS

> 2 eggs, hard-cooked
> mayonnaise (see index)
> 4 slices buttered toast
> 2 tomatoes
> 4 stuffed olives

METHOD: Shell and halve the eggs horizontally; remove yolks, mash with a little well-seasoned mayonnaise, and stuff the whites with this mixture. Remove a small slice from the bottom of each half-white so that the stuffed egg will stand upright.

Cut four little rounds from the buttered toast; cover each with a thick slice of tomato, stand the eggs on the tomato, and plant a stuffed olive in the centre of each filling. Serves 4.

CROÛTONS AU JAMBON

> 1 shallot
> 1 tablespoon butter
> 1 cup minced ham
> 2 egg yolks
> 1 tablespoon cream
> salt and pepper
> croûtes (see index)
> ½ teaspoon chopped parsley

METHOD: Chop shallot finely and sauté in the butter until lightly browned; add ham and stir over low heat until shallot is soft. Now stir in the egg yolks slowly, then the cream; season with a little pepper and pinch of salt. Stir over heat until mixture thickens, but do not let it boil. Pile the mixture on the croûtes, sprinkle with the parsley, and serve. Serves 8.

SARDINES AUX OEUFS

4 eggs, hard-cooked
4 tinned sardines
1 teaspoon anchovy paste
2 tablespoons béchamel sauce (see index)
salt and pepper
2 teaspoons chopped pickled gherkins
sprigs of watercress

METHOD: Shell eggs and cut in half; trim off bases to enable them to stand firmly. Carefully remove yolks. Chop sardines coarsely and pound them with the yolks, adding the anchovy paste and béchamel sauce; season to taste and rub through a sieve; add gherkins. Put into the white-of-egg cases and stand the egg halves upright. Garnish with watercress. Serves 4.

CAKES

My method of making sponges or light cakes may
horrify some people because I always beat the mixture with
my bare hands: this makes the cakes much lighter—something, I think, to do with the natural warmth of hands. As I
am continually washing my hands in the course of my work,
there is nothing unhygienic in this.

SAND TORTE

1 cup (½ lb.) butter
1 cup sugar
4 eggs
1 cup flour
¼ cup rice flour
1 heaping teaspoon baking powder
½ cup cornstarch
grated rind of ½ orange

METHOD: Preheat oven to 300°. Butter a shallow 10-inch cake pan. Cream butter and sugar and add eggs one by one. Add the other ingredients lightly; mix well together, but be careful to stir gently. Pour into the pan and bake for 1½ hours. Serves 6.

CHOCOLATE CAKE

½ lb. shortbread cookies
½ cup butter
1 tablespoon raisins
4 tablespoons cocoa
1 tablespoon chopped walnuts
1 tablespoon maple syrup
a few drops Curaçao
1 square semisweet chocolate, coarsely grated

METHOD: Roughly break up the cookies in a mixing bowl. Put butter in a pan and melt over low heat; remove and add raisins, cocoa, walnuts, maple syrup, and Curaçao. Stir the mixture into the broken cookies. Oil a shallow cake pan 6 or 7 inches wide, with detachable base. Fill this with the mixture, pressing it down and flattening it evenly. Put into refrigerator for 4 hours or until well set. Turn out on a serving dish and sprinkle with coarsely grated chocolate. Cut into pieces before serving. Serves 6 to 8.

RUSSIAN GÂTEAU

> ½ cup butter
> 1 cup sugar
> 3 eggs
> 2 cups self-raising flour, sifted
> 1 tablespoon ground almonds
> a little milk
> a few drops raspberry flavouring
> cochineal for colouring
> 2 teaspoons cocoa
> a few drops vanilla extract

METHOD: Preheat oven to 375°. Butter an oblong loaf pan and line it with waxed paper. Cream butter and sugar until fluffy; beat the eggs and add. Gradually stir in the flour, add the ground almonds, and mix well, adding a little milk if necessary. Put a third of the mixture into a bowl, mix in a few drops of raspberry flavouring, and colour this until light pink with a few drops of cochineal. Put half the remainder of the mixture into another bowl. Mix in cocoa and flavour with a few drops of vanilla. Leave the remaining uncoloured mixture as it is. Pour into the pan, a little at a time, batter from each of the three bowls, so that the colours are well blended. Bake for 1 hour. Remove from pan and cool on a wire rack. When the cake is cold, make marzipan icing and completely cover the cake on top and sides.

MARZIPAN ICING

> 1 cup ground almonds
> ½ cup finely granulated sugar
> ¾ cup confectioner's sugar
> ½ teaspoon vanilla extract
> juice of ½ lemon
> yolk of 1 egg

METHOD: Mix dry ingredients well; add vanilla and lemon juice, then the egg yolk. Knead thoroughly until smooth.

ALMOND CAKE

½ cup butter
⅔ cup finely granulated sugar
½ cup ground almonds
3 eggs
⅓ cup self-raising flour, sifted
confectioner's sugar

METHOD: Preheat oven to 350°. Cream the butter, add the sugar, and beat until white. Add the ground almonds; beat the eggs and add with the flour. Butter and lightly flour a shallow 10-inch cake pan. Fill with the mixture and bake 35 to 40 minutes, or until the cake comes away from the side of the pan. Turn out, cool, and dust with confectioner's sugar.

A French lady's maid gave me this recipe; she came to visit at a house where I was cook, a large house tucked away in a park quite near Southampton Water. At night I could look out of my kitchen and see the lights twinkling across the water.

I was designated the "lady chef," and my position was one of unusual trust because when my employer went away, which was frequently, she would put me in charge of her teen-age daughter, whom I will call Helen. It was a responsibility, as Helen was a high-spirited girl, as pretty as her mother, and in the evenings she kept disappearing; I could seldom find her for the evening meal. At last I said I should have to tell her mother—I had guessed there was a young gentleman farmer in the case—and that night, on going to my bedroom, I found hanging on the latch a gold bracelet adorned with charms. I took it straight away to Helen and told her I was not "open" to things like that and I should telephone her mother next day. She promised to behave, and kept her promise, for she was a nice child. She could be resentful at my anxiety and concern, though, and used to start singing the then popular song, "Olga Palofski, the beautiful spy," which made the servants laugh; but she could be as sweet as she was naughty, and we became real friends—which brings me back to the almond cake.

Helen was very, very fond of almond cake, and when I made it for her she would ask me up to tea in her sitting-room, which had everything in it a girl could wish for: white furnishings, a white piano, a royal-blue carpet—with an adorable white Pekingese, Mitzi, lying on it. (I seem always to be dogged—if you will forgive the pun—by Pekingese; my mother used to breed them, and I have had them all my life.) Helen would be most charming on these occasions and we would talk—I was quite young then—and eat my almond cake, and then she would reward me by playing Gershwin's "Rhapsody in Blue" for me; it used to fascinate me so much I could have forgiven her anything.

GINGER CAKE

½ cup butter
1 cup brown sugar
2 eggs
1 cup molasses
2 cups self-raising flour
¼ cup raisins
1 teaspoon ground ginger
¼ cup sliced preserved ginger
½ teaspoon baking soda
2½ tablespoons milk

METHOD: Preheat oven to 350°. Cream the butter, add the sugar, and cream again well. Beat in the eggs and add the molasses. Mix in the flour, raisins, ground ginger, and preserved ginger. Warm the baking soda in the milk and add to the mixture. Butter and lightly flour an oblong loaf pan; pour the mixture in, and bake for 1½ to 2 hours. Turn out onto a wire rack and cool.

MRS. MANDERS' CHRISTMAS CAKE

1 cup (½ lb.) butter
1⅔ cup brown sugar
5 eggs
2 teaspoons molasses
1½ cups seedless raisins
¾ cup mixed dried fruit peel
¾ cup glacé cherries
1½ cups dried currants
1 cup seeded raisins
½ cup ground almonds
2 tablespoons allspice
½ teaspoon salt
3 cups self-raising flour
⅓ cup brandy

METHOD: Preheat oven to 300°. Cream butter and sugar. Add eggs singly, beating each one in well. Add molasses. Mix the prepared fruit and nuts with the allspice and flour. Mix well together and stir into the creamed butter-and-egg mixture. Add the brandy and mix thoroughly. Butter a 10-inch cake pan, 4 inches deep, and pour in the batter. Bake 3 hours.

The longer this cake is kept, the better it is; make it at least three weeks before Christmas.

MELTING MOMENTS

¾ cup butter or margarine
⅓ cup sugar
2 eggs
2 cups cornstarch
1 teaspoon baking powder
¼ teaspoon vanilla extract

METHOD: Preheat oven to 350°. Cream butter and sugar together. Beat the eggs well and add, with the cornstarch and baking powder. Finally add a few drops of vanilla and mix well. Grease small patty tins and spoon mixture into them. Bake for 20 minutes.

EPILOGUE

". . . to my judges make this one protest:
A poor performance, but—I did my best."

INDEX